I0027673

Anonymous

Confused Characters of Conceited Coxcombs

A Dish of Traitorous Tyrants

Anonymous

Confused Characters of Conceited Coxcombs
A Dish of Traitorous Tyrants

ISBN/EAN: 9783337253028

Printed in Europe, USA, Canada, Australia, Japan

Cover: Foto ©Thomas Meinert / pixelio.de

More available books at **www.hansebooks.com**

Confused Characters

OF

CONCEITED COXCOMBS,

OR,

A DISH OF TRAITOROUS TYRANTS;

REPRINTED FROM

THE ORIGINAL EDITION OF A.D. 1661.

EDITED BY

JAMES O. HALLIWELL, ESQ., F.R.S.

LONDON:

PRINTED BY THOMAS RICHARDS,

37, GREAT QUEEN STREET.

1860.

PREFACE.

ALL the books of characters of the seventeenth century are curious, and include important illustrations of our early manners and customs ; and few, of a date after the restoration of Charles the Second, are more intrinsically valuable and interesting than the little volume now reprinted. It is, indeed, one of the few, belonging to a comparatively late period, which partakes of the character of the earlier works of the same class. The name of the author is unknown, but his initials are ascertained from the title of the copy of verses addressed by a friend " to his much esteemed friend K. W. congratulating his Characters." There can be but little doubt that he belonged to one of the universities ; and, most probably, to that of Cambridge. At least, this may be conjectured from the verses entitled,

"A Petition of Questionests to Mr. Frost for their degrees, Woodcock and Heron Procters." There was a John Frost of Cambridge, whose sermons were published in the year 1658, and who is perhaps the individual here referred to. The following list of characters in the reprint now made will be useful for reference, and indeed it is difficult to add more preface of any value to a republication of this kind, in a case where no particulars are known respecting either the author or his work,—

1. A Courtier. P. 19.
2. A Conceited Statesman. P. 23.
3. A Meere Polititian. P. 25.
4. An Upstart Pragmaticall. P. 29.
5. A Justice of Peace. P. 32.
6. A High Constable. P. 34.
7. A Juryman Rustick. P. 36.
8. A Church-Warden. P. 38.
9. A Baily or Serjeant. P. 39.
10. A Lawyer in Common. P. 42.
11. An Informer. P. 44.
12. A Flatterer. P. 48.
13. A Temporizer. P. 50.

Amongst the more curious allusions may be mentioned those to the mouth of Aldersgate; Noll's, or Oliver Cromwell's countenance; Joan Cromwell asking the Dutchess of Albemarle how her children's portions should be raised; patches on lady's faces; a coin called St. George; Hyde Park, Spring Gardens, and Mulberry Gardens; the drolleries of Sir Thomas Martin; Alderman Atkins; the eels of Cheapside; Islington cake-house; Bartholomew Fair; etc.

Since noting the above, I observe an allusion proving to which university the author belonged,—" Never, till I was at Cambridge, did I see the logician's chimæra," etc.

CONFUSED

CHARACTERS

of Conceited

Coxcombs:

OR,

A Dish of Trayterous

Tyrants, dressed with Verjuice and
pickeled too posterity.

*Together with their Camp-retinue and
Fems Covert.*

By *Verax Philobasileus.*

Integer vitæ scelerisque purus,
Non eget Mauri jaculis, nec arcu
Nec venenatis gravida sagittis,·
  Phusce, pharetra.

London, Printed by *T. M.* for *Typographus*
at the Signe of the World, 1661.

Facecious Reader,

CHARACTERS are descriptions, and where the persons described prove vitious and vain, excuse me, gentle reader, if this treatise prove so likewise. The laborious bee by nice chymistry extracts the elixar of her thime, and loads her feeble thighes with yellow sweetnesse, though perhaps the nettle, or other ranck flower, be her subject: and I should wrong your judgments with censorious severity, should I think so bad of you, as but to suppose otherwise, then that your penetrating and perforating intellectuals will extract some honey from this aloes. Should I, like an unthrifty cobler, have underlayed the rotten soles of these now worn out buskings, with the new and costly leather of applause, and sticht them up with the ends of commendation, the subject would not have born it: and I my self had played the parasite, and it had been *Sutor ultro crepidam.* Should I with Neroes courtiers have wringed the neck of my discourse awry, and distorted it to a clawing dialect: I might have well deserved the fate of Dyonisius his sycophants, and have been bound to a continuall ingurgitation of their spittle for drink and nourishment. *Semel insanivimus omnes,* saith that poet : and sure, then, their mad actions may be part of an excuse for my hairbraind undertakings.   And since many of them received pardon of their outrages, committed on regiment and order, let me sue out my pardon of those more enormous affronts, I have put upon sense and ingenuity.   Indeed, the witty saying of a gentleman was then most true : that in England we had not clergic men enough, gentlemen enough, nor Jews enough.   Clergic men we had scarce any ; there were many extended jaws, gaping as the mouth at Aldersgate, and belching forth schisme, but no well ordained divines, scarce tollerated : our gentlemen were περίζυμα τῆς γῆς, of the same generation with frogs, toads, and field mice, formed of the slime and dirt of the nation ; and animated by the heat of that sun which was placed in the center of Nols meridian countenance. Never was boorish inhumanity so much in fashion, never upstart pride more common ; and these beggars getting on horseback, shew'd the world a new way, how with more speed to ride to the devill. We had not Jews enough neither, for they should by all means have had a tolleration ; because ten in the hundred was out of fashion, and the art of cheating was not sufficiently practised. These things thus considered, I care not if I play the foole too ; and since they are wanting, supply the place, and stile myself Englands jack pudding. I have good store of impudence (which I procured of the magazine which Jone had, when she was so religiously bashfull, as to ask the dutches of Albemarle, how her childrens portions which old Noll left them should be raised?) And I care not, for neither shall you put me out of countenance with all your dislikes, and comments, and paraphrases, &c. ; for if you do not approve, cast your eyes off to what your humour fancies more accurately. And for pride, let me alone to scorn all your sayings ; Pride, by name and nature too, was my sedulous tutor. And as for the foolery I spoke off, I have a sufficient example in Harry the nineth, S. Richard the fourth ; for where as we use alwayes to say Tom-fool, and Tom-as ; they have lately petitioned his majestie, that reverent title may be shown by their coats, and that they for ever may be accounted the patrons and magnificent champions of that ridiculous and thrice merry sect and association. Thus, gentle reader, being accoutred, I fear not your batteries. But I doubt, should this pamphlet meet with the ghost of St. Harrison, it would grow pale with amazement, and be quite out of countenance. And truely now I speak of him, they say Peters upbraids him extreamly, because being alive, he condemned all civil judicatures, now being dead, he countenances the whole bench, and out faces the whole tribe of lawyers ; and alwayes stayes last in the Hall. Harrison affirms the contrary, and sayes its out of zeale to the good old cause his quondam strumpet (with whom he so often committed fornication) for since he cannot speake to them in contempt, nor bite them in revenge, he's zealously resolved to shew his teeth and grin at them, if by any means he may affright them. And truly as they did not well accord living, so now, the living and the dead fall out and law it accordingly. Titchburn, that namesake of Tibourn, which as there's but two letters difference; so there's scarce two steps between him and the fate of being a knight of the three corner'd cap: this cathern jaw'd elfe, pines at the great disparity between Hugh Peters beard and his; and hath sued him in hels chancery for his legacy; he should have sent him from Charing Crosse, viz., his beard. Rhadamanthus (that is, Bradshaw), is the umpire in the nicety, and Hugh pleades he hath drunk Lethe and forgot it. Whereupon the president dismist them with councell first for the plaintiff, sent to him by Gaffar Lenthall and Oliver St. Johns, the two letter-carriers between the *quandam* halter-man and him, viz. I will and require thee, O thou faint-hearted dildo, to rest satisfied till thy turn comes, and thy exaltation is at hand; and then by vertue of the mists of Thamesis and its uncteous vapours thou shalt fructify in the jaw to so great a plenitude, that by Lammas it may be mowen, and sold to the plasterers to binde their mortar. To Hugh thus he thundred, Oh thou impe of ignorance and weesell of wit, boast not thy self of thy bristled turnpikes, lay but thy hand upon thy crown, and thou shalt feele the effects of the butchers wife ; boast not therefore least thy jaws be singed.

There was lately (courteous reader) a great and solemn meeting of the three grand rebbels of this nation ; how their bodies were animated and enlivened judge you : but they all met, and afterwards in a solemn manner laid their heads together, from whence some dangerous, very dangerous plot and disaster may be expected. I shall treat of them in their order : the first that appeared was one who in his traiterous prosperity would have scared the devil, and have vyed fires with hell it self with his complexion ; but now appearing offended not the eye so much as the nose, and by stench and noisome vapours proclaimed a state, and the supremacy of a *Noli me tangere*, I pray you stand off. Thus doe troublesome and obnoxious persons equally disturbe in all dispensations alive. None but those bastard eagles, whose hardy and unrelenting opticks could gaze on, and rejoyce over the hideously murdered corps of a gracious and thrice blessed prince : none of such birds of prey were able to withstand the confounding rayes and sulphurus beams of his ominall countenance, which affrighted all loyall and natural eyes, as if they had been plannet-struck : dead. None but collegiates in the same infernall residence, were able to breath in that fatall aire which he had corrupted : those excepted, whose extasied souls ravished with joy of his condigne punishment, by excesse of exalted spirits did themselves injuries, rather then omit the sight of so perfidious a monster. So that alive, he offended the eyes with his nose ; dead, he afflicted the nose for the eyes curiosity. The second was a limbe of the same feind, his son in law, a man as bad as himself in desires, though the great devil kept his equall under, one that lost his life, because he never found the true use of it ; a man of approved mettle and mischief, and for his perpetual infamy, one of Nols nymphs. The third a piece of lack latine, a lawyer who experimentally knew a tenure in *capite* by grand serjeanty near Paddington. A man of learning, and a second Dr. Faustus, though he rendred all but himself infelices most miserable : a president to follow whose example did necessarily include perdition : a president whose brazen front feared not impiously to condemn his sovereign and martyr his king. And to summe up all, one that made religion a cloake to shrow'd all villanies and conceale them. The first, had his gifts been graces, might have attained the honor of an Albemarle, and eternized his name with honourable titles, more glorious than infamous : and the rest of his helhounds, had not they hunted counter and confusedly, might have catcht the haire of order, and obtained the game of discipline, and then would the world have shouted. and ecchoed forth their praises and commendations, These had their grand meeting at a convenient place, convenient for its figure, each man his corner ; convenient for its scituation in a by and mischievous place ; convenient for its use, a place befitting their deserts, and suiting their treason. But being scared somewhat, they resolved to lay their joult-heads together, and the place of meeting was under a dust basket, where being something stounded at the treatment, sued an exaltation. These three me thinks are the morrall of Cerberus ; and were indeed the hellish porters too let in confusion into the land ; and I believe have the sop of reward by this time abundantly bestowed upon them.

Something may be said of them as of Maximus ; they were valiant and victorious, but tyrannicall usurpation and murderous regicidation spoiled the markets of their swelling honour, and poisoned their names with the guilt of perjury. Then Apollonius Thianæus his experiment, that he in his travels observed, was abundantly verified, for the proud then did command the humble, the quarrellous the quiet, the tyrant the just : and the greatest thieves and most detestable murderous hang the innocent. It was asked one what exploits he had done in the Low Countries ? O, quoth he, I cut of a Spanyards legs. Reply being made, it had been something if he had cut off his head : Oh, saith he, you must consider the head was off before. But these impious scoundrels first made a decollation, and deprived us of the blessed head of our body politick, and afterwards cut off the legs too, and altogether left it a mishapen trunk, exanimate and deformed. But thus much for my apology, for some of my first essayes ; if a Hide Park lady chance to be offended with any thing, she may think concerns her honour ; all I can say to such monsters, who when nature hath given

them but one spot, affects an hundred, and set the
fashion of their secrets in their faces without blushing :
all that I shall say to them, is what one said of scan-
dals. If I do not deserve, saith he, what is thrown
upon me, my life will give them the lye : if I do, its
my duety to be patient and amend : if, ladyes, your
vertuous modesty vyes splendour with your faces, and
ingenuity be as prevalent as beauty, then I rejoyce to
finde an exception from the general rule, and to be
proved a lyar ; but if rampish lust and damnable
pride, in marring what God made, and making your
selves party per pale blackmores in part, in part English : if the insatiable appetite must have the conveni-
ency of gallants, and new sorts of impieties are found
out for titillation and sodomy, pardon me then if I
guesse at your lives, and tell your faults. As for those
covetous misers, and scraping hags, whose fate it is to
grovell in minerals, till the damp of death saves the
hangman a labor : all I shall accost them with, is what
naturalists observe of these countries where gold mines
are plentifull ; the ground is alwaies barren and unfruitfull. So say I to you, *Quid non mortalia pectora*

cogit? Auri sacra famos. This greedy worm of much desire will seduce thee to most impieous enormities, and render thy soule unfruitfull of the least goodness. But I shall make the porch bigger then the house if I proceed any further; I shall therefore desire you to look upon these fooleries, as the diversions of a solitary life, and as the refreshments of a young brain in these sad dayes, when government lay a bleeding, and loyalty was accounted frency. And let the carping reader mend what he sees amiss in these puerrill exercises, and he that cannot better it, let him learn to hold his peace : if any like it, I am content ; if no body are pleased, I am still content, and will be in spight of the most criticall judgements ; and so adieu.

To his much esteemed friend *K. W.*
Congratulating his Characters.

CEASE, *cease, you scribling puny pamphleteeres ;*
 See here a more elustrious pen appeares ;
Poore pedling poetasters, you may scoule,
And weeping Polyhymne may go howle :
Your markets spoil'd, but if you needs must use
Your wonted trade, send out some backey muse,
On Pegasus in post to tell about,
That late, a new borne star hath been found out :
Wits comits therefore, now snuff out the blaze,
On which the vulgar so with wonder gaze ;
Send home your borrowed vapours, and restore
That light, by which you shin'd so bright before.
This new rise planet, with his infant light,
Out shines you all, being mounted at your height.
O then, if by the dawning we may guesse,
Of the insuing day, what happynesse

Will thy high noon produce, thou needs must bring
A fruitfull summer, but so good a spring.
And if in prentiship thou thus erect,
Thou sure at last must be wits architect.

L. G.   A. C. C.

To the Ladies.

SHORT *hand and characters in sense agree,*
  Then what care I (sweet ladies) if you see
Your selves epitomiz'd? You'd blush I'me sure
Should I tell all, and not the light endure.
Ciphers are characters, and you, I know,
Do love to have your I turn'd to an O.
And think it no unhappy cipher when,
Circles and figures are made out by men ;
And say it makes a summe, because your I
Was set before the O's supremacy.
Say not that 'cause of shortness I do err,
Since you'r decypherd in a character.
You ladies, long and large I know do fancy,
But not reproofs ; but such things as did Nanse
Praise in Hide-Parke and wish for, when she see
The fifth leg of a stone-horse rampant t' be ;
Therefore to you I'e scarce direct my stuff,
You brevity despise and hate reproof.

K. W.

CHARACTERS.

COURTIER is one of Apuleius's golden asses, whose fine cloths hang about his body as the painted cloth before the men that act a puppet play ; only to abscond, and vail his simplicity from the eyes of the vulgar, and to put a seeming shew of generosity in his garments and habiliment : though in truth and verity he's but a meer gew-gaw. He is one of Æsops fable verified ; proud, prick-eard, fillies, masqued in the gorgeous and majestick attire of an heroical lyon ; for though he bridles it, and looks aloft on those he calls the inferior (*i. e.*, those that have not as fantasticall an attire as himself), yet he himself, *infra*, beneath or rather within his gay *antimasq :* (I mean in his intellectuals and internal accomplishments), is as pittifull a piece of mortality, if he once comes to the exercise of the minde, as that lazie tinker who (is reported to have) layed down his wallet to ——— ! But lets trace him a little, and follow him from his forme or nest. The first step he takes is, it may be, to the university, whether his good old syre sends him, to store himself with solid and substantiall erudition, though he only prankes up his fancy with the swelling title (of fellow-commoner)

because the first aspect of his velvet is a cogent argument to obtain freeness of accesse to his landresse or butlers daughter, or other town doxies. And its upon them, and to redeem their favor, and purchase a smile from them, that he sends so many St. Georges to an eternal errantry never to returne to his burnt bottometh pocked. These he reverenceth with the title of faire lady, as he doth the court minions (those paramours of lust, and inveaghlers to debauchery) with his now more affected and modish congratulations. His tutor perhaps takes paines with him in his logick, but he neither can nor will understand any term but that of a non entity, because he is conscious to himself he's no schollar. A thought of *smagletius* terrifies and affrights him as much as *compossibilitas* and *incompossibilitas* did noble Randolphs simplicius; perhaps if he be somewhat of Balams temper, that would be accounted a good conjurer, but wo'nt take pains, then he steeps and souseth his memory with a few hard words and broken sentences, and thereby gets and obtains his end, viz., the reputation of a good schollar amongst his fellows; that do as much fear the rattling discord of such harsh sounding, noddle puzling sequepedalian words, as ever that white-liver'd monarch did thunder, or as the slattering of a cadent brickbat. Here also he learns to buss his hand, make a leg, pluck off the hat, and to go aloof off, of the fashion; to be impudent, court a strumpet methodically, and that without the former ruine of his buttons and bandstrings, to be drunk, sing and roare out bawdy catches, and then by this time, he's fit for Grayes Inn, or some other inns of court.

Now his father sends for him home, thinking his son to be a good proficient, when he's in the same form with that storied lack latting that invented the upstart Latine of *Stonum bonum crowpeckaweedum.* Well, after he hath made his fathers man drunk, and the rest of the company merry, he obeys his fathers injunctions, and up rides he to London the next term to be initiated at the inns of court and throw away five pounds. And now he begins to get a step higher.

Here he meets with some of his *quondam* acquaintance, and then march they, and enter him in a bawdyhouse, where after he hath been well squeezed in his pockets by the Hectors, he begins to learn some policy in wickednesse : he mindes nothing lesse than Littleton, and can show no tenure of his wit, but that he hath it a fee-simple. He thinks it a mode to come home late drunk, and so to quarrel and gets his pate broken ; and by that means he knows what it is to hold in *capite.* He gets the French cranckums, and so knows what it is to have a tenure in *taile.* He games himself into debt, and rants himself into pawnings, and by an arrest and forfeiture, knows the nature of petty serjeants and a mortgage. Thus he runs divisions upon Sr. Edward Cook, by experimental annota-

tions. This long since he did begins, *Patrios inqui-*
rere in annos, thinking in his heart it is a sin for any
father to live after his eldest son is twenty one, and
now it may be by this time, the old man takes an
occasion to march off and depart. And then my gentleman gets him a wife *procreandi causa,* and comes
up to London, and turns courtier, or as it commonly
happens, turns no better then stallion for other mens
ladies, as other men do for his. Now his lust is at the
height, and his pride hath its *ne plus ultra.* His onely
work is to set the tailor on work; for his allwayes a
translating his suits, and loves to show himself sin-
gular in his fancies. He adores his minnions trophies
or rump knots more than God, and fears the want of
erection and warm blood more then the devill, and that
makes him so duellize and quarrell for the one, and
take such provocative in censitive medicines for the
other. In the winter cards, dice, balls and venery, are
his religion and recreation; but in all gaming, he
thinks he's bound to loose if his pursse plays against
him. In the spring, my lady and her leaper hurry to
Hide-park, and then my ruffling gallant turns coach-
man, and hurries her to the lodge, Spring-gardens and
Mulbury-gardens, and there they frolick it a little, and
so to prick-penny. And now he is at the height of
his atchievements, and if he can but gain the art of
flattering, or colloguing, he thinks himself the best man
in Christendome. After all his wilde oats are well

sown, and his wife hath well loaded him with bearns, he begins to grow a little more serious, and then his aimes may be towards state affairs, and his designes are to insinuate into such a place of dignity as he may be called a statesman, but you'ld guesse him a conceited one.

A conceited Statesman.

A CONCEITED statesman is one that thinks more of himself than others dare ; and the higher he thinks to soare in the opinion of the multitude, the more he unvailes his own imbecility, and renders himself pellucid ; his state maximes are as few as his designes, and they come just to nothing ; for all his aym is to make a show in the world, and so he doth, though it is but a foolish one. When he sits in consultation, he knows not how to drive away the time, but by nodding, and by his sleep makes it manifest, he is silently consulting with his pillow, if he chances to put in a word by the by ; for he speaks in a parenthesis, he doth it with a great deale of deliberation, so to make men imagine the matter to be weighty and of importance ; when, alasse! it is onely to pick out a little sense out of his nonsensicall imaginations. So that it may be said of all his productions,

Parturiunt montes, nascetur ridiculus mus.

For like that cardinals stately sumpture-horses lading, though he may promise some policy in his feigned aspect, yet when by chance he overthrows the burden of his thoughts by an oration (which is an offence to him), he discovers the old shoes and empty marribones of his barren pericranium. Other mens speeches and motions he never minds; for his watch, his gold fringed gloves and sowre faces, take up all the time.

If he hath any traffique or dealing with his superiours, his conceited coxcomb vents its own simplicity without interrogation, for by his affected studiousness to seem grave and prudent, he renders his unpollisht and incult intellect more conspicuous. If his discourse be with an equal, then, by thinking himself the best man in the company, he shows he hath quite forgot, or never read, the first great consideration of a statesman (viz., *cognoscere seipsum*), for he whose aspiring mind will not condiscend to the thoughts of its own state, will never have brains enough to consider of any thing that is or may be apparently good for a state or kingdome. If his inferiours are with him, he vents other mens motions for his own, and some of his own too if he can remember them ; and never concludes with out a self applause, viz., was it not a good motion ? Now he bewrays his ignorance in policy, by declaring state-councels to the vulgar, whose conceits of politique notions are as crude and raw as his own. And though he may think himself fit to be a privy counseller, yet for my part I think him a fitter man to be councellor in a privy. If he rides down into the country, he makes the silly swaines there adore him as a god, whom indeed they may esteem beneath a man ; and when death comes, all that he leaves behinde him signifies but thus much 0 ; viz., a cypher.

A meere Polititian

IS one whom, if one should trace from the beginning, we might finde him a man of good parts, though of low condition ; one of a sharp wit, contriving head piece, resolute minde, strong body and constitution, though the first is blunted for lack of exercise, the second scanted for lack of matter, the third and fourth augmented by want and experience : some of these have been so ingenious as to hammer alls into rapiers, lasts into lists, neats leather into buff-coats, and themselves out of a narrow stall into a spacious field in the head of an army. Others, by continual use of brasse, have so brazed their faces and steeled their consciences, that they shame not to use pole axes in lieu of hammers ; and to make the tinkers character true indeed, viz., under a pretence of mending the holes and crevices of a decayed state, have rended and cloven in sunder a whole republique. Others, by the vertue of

E

malt, have acquired such an excellent faculty, that
they can sling a state into a new *de corum*; and after
a purging and cleansing of (as they pretend) the musty
cask of a kingdome, bung it up with the salt and clay
of a commonwealth and lord protector. And all or
any of them (by this time) have learnt the trade of
policies, and therefore we show their acquired experimental principals. Their first principall apparent (and
truly that is all) (after they have winded themselves
up to this pitch of credit, and have got the hosanna of
the vulgar) is the good, the spiritual good of the republique; and here they follow the example of repairers,
who pull down for edification. And the former good,
old, wholesome, rites and customes, not onely of a
nation in generall, but also of all reformed churches,
according to the Apostolical Faith, must be brought
under the notion of superstition and idolatry. Now
these politique moles begin to cast up the solid mold
of religion into loose and discontinued heaps of consci-
entius liberty; that so this, like one of the devils
moustraps, may allure the pillidging mice of a state to
complyance in wickednesse.

Now the mask of all their proceeding is reformation;
i. e., to reduce a nation into their power, unto their
bow. The Bible is the standard of their actions, till
politique necessity forces their feigned reality to a
disobedience.

A second principall is flattery and colloguing with

all parties ; promising mountains, but performing
nought but such mole-hill actions as breed and produce
nothing but a multitude of pissants and vermins of his
own constitution. Now, by his over much seeming
affability, he shews his servill and ignoble nature :
which will do any thing to procure it self a sound of
fame, which will availe him little ; but to be an *indi-
cium* of his own vacuity and emptiness of all sollidity ;
and his repliatnesse of insippid aierial and light whim-
sies. Promised preferment is all his reward to them
perhaps, who deserve better than himself.

But his third principall, is to lay by (either by pick-
ing a quarrell with, or devising plots against) such as
have been his coadjutors to this commetique serenity.
And now he begins to play the devill on earth, who if
he mends not his manners, may work with the devill
in hell. By fasting, he ripens his wits to contrive
plots ; and when this is done, he draws in the rich and
wealthy of the nation, by his promoters, and thinks
now to make his sequestration and forfeiture lawfull in
the eyes of the vulgar. He gives thanks for his good
success in these tyrannical conceipts, under pretence of
gratitude, for a deliverance : and so it is ; for by this
means, viz. by cheating and trappanning others of their
estates, he delivers his children and kinsmen from
their naturall slavery and wonted beggery. *Unum pro
multis dabitur caput*, is another rule and his best to, if
he knew how to use it as he should, but that is in-

flicted upon the innocent : and those whose crimes are as red as his nose (for that cannot but reflect the colour of that bloud he hath spilt) go not only scot-free, but rewarded also and advanced.

He now is a pure free-man, only he is a little over-swayed with the voluminous bulke of that army, whose idle lives hate the mention of a revertion to their wonted druggery. These he maintains, not with his purse, but by his wits ; and by his taxes lays himself liable to be taxed of tyranny, and at the end levies his own ruine.

He never makes conscience of any former protestations, but seing his body decayed, thinks to establish other mens labours on his own progeny, and just before he hath done councelling his wilde son, he is blown away with a blast, and the snuff of his life will stink this twelve mouths.

This is the head generall polititian ; private ones differ only in degrees. To undermind competitors for the same place is one designe, and thus they do by dawbing over their stinking conditions to their superiours with the specious shew of humility and devotion : and by threatning or alluring their inferiors into a compliance (by their acclamations) to their designs having once got his head into the rising clymate never leaves winding his muddy head-piece, to an aspiring higher, till he it may be grows shorter by the head, and takes the recompence of his knavery on a block.

And there we'l leave him, least further anatomizing his politicall body, we discharge such a stench of iniquity as may new seal an honest and well meaning stomack.

An Upstart Pragmaticall.

A Parliament man is one who hath turn'd his leather brecks into the new fashion; and because he hath squeesed an estate out of the ruines of superiors, and nourished his lean carcase by the blood of his betters, thinks he is a man sufficient to sit at the starne of a commonwealth, but scarce knows which way to steare, only by his hands those naturall informers; and its well to, if he knows his right hand from his left. His ambition to be great makes his simple noddle shew its sottishnesse in publique, whereas if the squire and no gentleman, would have contented himself with a justice of peaceship and good house-keeping, he might have been made (by the help of a good clarke) passable in the eye of the country.

He is so farr from that good Athenians temper, who rejoyced there were many that deserved preferment better then himself, that he thinks himself the only man for the place, and all others in comparison of him are but like a pismire to an elephant. You shall finde him speaking the neighbouring towns from their voices in affected course complements, just raked from the

plow taile and bedaubed with new terms and eloquent
(as he accounts them) phrases, and on the election day
in coms Tobit and his dogs following him ; for I know
none but animals will vote for one whose wit cannot
be compared to some infectiles.   He much assimulates
the Sarazens head without Newgate, when his brawny
bum is set upon his mens shoulders ; his face being
swelled with the immagination of a chaire of state ; he
carries an aspect like a town bull, or a full necked
presbyter.   Now if these fools should chance to let the
asse paramount salute his mother earth with his vener-
able buttocks, it may well be said, like will to like, as
the devill to the colliar.

The greatest opposition to this his designe, is the
fast he must keep at Westminster ; for there he fears an
insurrection in his belly, and dare not stuffe his greasy
pokets with flotten cheese, for fear of the hogoe, and
his wonted enemy the rats.   The first day, the man is
so amazed at the new convention, and so unskilfull in
the art of policy, that he takes a resolution to do no
good, because he cannot speak sence ; and you may
trust him, he hath not wit enough to do harme.

But after the newnesse of the thing grows common,
and his ignorant impudence begins to take place, then
who so forward as master Upstart ; for he cannot tell
what though he aimes at nothing but contradiction,
and will hammer out a negative, though he knows not
the meaning of an affirmative.   He's so far from being

sensible of a scofe, that he thinks them commendations, and if any thing be done, straight he did it. He
may be compared to false ware, which your almost
bankrupt tradesmen use in their shops (rags hansomly
tied up as their other) to make a shew, but are never
used ; so he takes up the roome of those whose good
parts and education give them a lawfull claime to the
place. If he makes a speech it is a 12. moneths study,
and if his mother went three quarters with him, he
may justly give his barren scull a fourth to conceive
and produce in : and its almost as long in speaking as
in preparing ; first ushered in with hems and wry
faces ; and farr more dangerous, for in making it, he
only threatned the ruine of one blockhead in speaking
of his buttons, beard, bandstrings, and handkercheifs,
a pittiful disjoyn'd peice of tautologie, when all is done,
whose incongruous matter can only unveile the mis-
carriages of a common nature by his own condition,
but knows no more how to prescribe a likely remedy,
then a childe or schoole boy : it may be and sure it is,
he doth think himself a rare prater, and so he might
have been accounted amongst the popet-players for his
widned throat, streacht with his former angry expostu-
lation with byard, and dobbing have extended the
noise of his organes even to the roaring gammut of a
martiall ; under pretence of religion, he sees his prag-
matical pate a working and reforming in the country.
Now all that will not worship the beast must downe

even to the ground. Those that comply with his humours, and none else shal thrive under his sphere ; and they are so many, that not only he of them but the house of him, and such others, lacks purging. He fears this more then hell, and would pine to death if he thought he should be outvoted the next election ; if he dies or is cast out, there is an end of him.

A Justice of Peace

IS one for the most part whose life runs antipodes to his name, and the name I believe was first founded upon an anteparistasis, for he hath not wit enough to do justice, and the clamours of his querulous neighbours will not let him live in peace and quietnesse. Lets take a view of him in his domestique affairs. You shall have his puney clarke (who because he swears others, thinks he may curse and lie by authority) ready to call him up to deside a two peny controversy, before he hath done his wife justice, which will make her break his peace if not his coxcombe. When he hath done with her, down he comes and hears two fools prate, and sends them with a few justices law notions, but no lawfull realities of justice. Hee's never so taken, and in his kingdom, as when the swearer or drunkard comes before him, then the informer must sweare, through an inch board at least, and then the

sots must either pay their money which he gapes at
(for he 'le be sure to threaten an unlawfull space of
time to pound them in) and then one groat goes to the
informer, one to the poor ; he keeps the other eight
pence for his pains, and so robs the poor, who fears his
worships frowns, and reverence him outwardly, but
curse him after.   He is never so hard matcht as when
he meets with an understanding yeoman and an impudent whore : the one puts him down by his reason
and experience in the law, the other by her impudence
and eloquent bawdry.   To her his wife listens ; and
may be will entreat for her fellow wanton, knowing
how hard a thing it is to live honestly.   At the quarter
sessions out rides his worship and his maker (for it is
the clarke makes the justice), where meeting with his
fellow simplicians, they license the most lycentious out
of policy of a future fine, and when alls done, like poor
schollers, whose moneys falls short, go a begging to
their clarks, whose onely wit is in their fingers ends
for a dinner, and ride home just asses as they came.
No wonder the judges are so carefull in their charges
on the bench to informe the justices of their duty ;
when few of them understand the law any better then
parrats, I, or ever knew the meaning of a præmuniry,
or other law term.   In a mittimus lyes their chiefest
skill ; and in a warrant they skill in the first two ways.
First, by being subtill to finde out and entrap rogues,
and this they do by their former practices; for what so

F

fit to unkennell a fox as the tarier which is or hath been a part of him ? Secondly, by being strict in the thing made, they will be sure to put in without baile or mainprise. The warrants they make and mittimus are repleat with many absurdities, all of kin to Sir Thomas Martin, and all big with the same drollerys. But I will leave him and his clarke (for they always go together, the justice being a cypher without him) to the croude and rabble, least speaking to much, we undo and defame that credit he never had.

A High Constable

IS a gentleman by his place, though not by his education and birth, for this his preferment hath metamorphosed the antient titles of his progeneters, viz. gaffer, and goodman, into master, and now he is vampt a gentleman, and got a butten hole higher then his forefathers ; his first step of honour was to be the head jury man of the great inquests, but in all his proceedings it's a *query* whether he understands the title. But whats the reason of this his first step, why ? Because he hath squeezed a *modicum* out of the bowels of his mother earth, which hath been a supplicate to his education, to teach his callous, and clumsy paw, the ill favoured demeanure of his penne to so great a proficiency, that he doth not now, as formerly, set his

marke, viz. a paire of galloes, or some such scawle, but
hath arrived to the mode of setting down his bald
name in his most mishapen illegable characters.

Now he begins to give up his verdict confidently
and ignorantly, and because his dirty face is not ca-
pable of a blush, except by the reflection of the judges
robes, he presumes to set himself in the place of the
company, and to be their mouth to the bench, who if
he were rightly examined, would be found to be a
meere mouth, *i. e.* a simplition. When the freeholder
comes to be chosen high constable, his excellency lies
in his account he can give of all the towns and parishes
in his wapentacke, and the under officers thereof (as
he calls them) the corporation towns of the shire and
their jurisdiction ; and this he doth to, after the
manner of that pitifull fresh water captaine, who was
to instruct his followers (for I cannot call them nor
him souldiers that were so raw in millitary discipline)
in warlike postures, and could not by reason of his in-
experience remember them : but at each command
looks on the paper pin'd on his skirt, and if his eye
chance to see double, he commands them to face about
to the wine mill.

So this shread of an officers members, I should had
said memory, being somewhat short, he will be sure to
keep up his old grandsires custome : viz. long and
large skirts, that so his skeld dole may make recompence to his memory for his short dimensions.

His place makes him come to church and heare, but a hundred to one his matted noddle is so stuft with the windy conceit of his mastership, that there's no room for any thing but adoration. Now his cuffs hang about his clumsy fists like dishclouts, made they are out of the ruines of his wifes smock; whose brawny bumm and course hide will soon freet out a piece of course lockrum. His cloak hangs on his shoulders much like a fidlers, only its somewhat fresher, and he fears to touch the sides on't, or give it a wispe under his arme, for fear his dirty clutch should grease it, and his wife scold at him for wrinkling his pontificalibus; but I fear a presentation next quarter sessions, therefore, good Mr. Gaffer, adieu.

A Juryman Rustick

THINKS his unhewen noddle able to give a rationall account of his charge, and place at the sizes of hisen prizes, as he call them, but alas! poor fellow, the latitude of his prickears show the whole world that they have suckt up his brains; and that his empty noddle is full of nought but conceit and self applause.

Did you but see him gape at the judge with his lockerum jaws, when he examines in the tryal, and gives his opinion, you would almost sweare either the sot hears with his mouth, or else the elve being a faint

hearted pupy sounds at the conceit he hath the judges
red robes are only the blood of some condemned
wretch. When he's retired to his considering plat, how
many frivolous nonsensical queris doth he make, and
when he brings in his verdict, he will be sure, either
becaus he would be thought a noble person, and so fit
for the place ; or else a prudent man, and so fit to be
regarded, he gives a sum of the costs and charges his
and their pitifull pates and indigent pericranium's
think equitable by nobles, or marks ; not by pounds,
because the threadbare scrub never saw at one time (of
his own) twenty shill. If he hath obtained to so high
a measure of book learednes (as he calls it) as to
write, then he's the best of the shire, and his leaden
pate serves to be the byasse of all his wooden headed
roundnodled associates, if his zeale pretended to religion, then after his verdict (as he calls it) he takes
upon him to informe the just-asses of the shire, of ill
licensed alehouses and other misdemenours, and thinks
thereby to have the credit to be accounted a man
respecting the republick good. But sizes being over,
hee's sure to have a parting blow ; I mean, a hogshead
of beer in his own asses noddle ; and then he gallops a
titering pace home, and the next day falls to repenting
for this (as he calls it) sin of infirmity.

Now he's turned a diurnal in folio, and as that doth,
he informs his neighbours of an abundance of lyes ;
which they are bound to believe, because he's one of

the twelve, and the twelfth wise man spoke it. Well, after he's prety well empty of all his stories, then to the plow again and his daily labour; and now he neither minds God nor the devill, only his mother earth; and he viper-like makes no conscience of piersing and penitrating his mothers bowels; but I fear my country men will be angry with me; but my best hope is that they cannot read, and then I hope I shall be free from their homespun execrations. However for a parting blow, master jury man, have a care of bribes and partiallity, interest and affection; for if you do the devills work hee'l be sure to pay your wages at your own sizes.

A Church-Warden.

A CHURCH-WARDEN may be compared to a choaky peare, which though grafted on never so good a stock, yet remains as bad and ill savoured as ever: so he by nature of a clownish and Nabal like temper; yet though he comes to the honour of the forementioned place, to be a warden or overseer of the church, yet he still retains his own naturall ignorance and stupidity. Yet neighbours, I hope, you'l respect Mr. church warden, for else hee'l be so farr from repairing and mending your meeting-place, as hee'l conspire your ruine in endeavouring its downfall. Well,

when all comes to all, he understands his place as
much as his wife, and she, as much as her daughter ;
and fools all, much alike ; if he chance to be of such a
publique spirit, as to new transmography his charge ;
then to be sure, he sets his name up in large characters ; as if he thought men were so much like him, as
to worship and adore such a pitifull piece of mortallity.
But woe be to his breeks when he gives up his accounts, which like that subtill Roman he seeks not to
do, rather then to do, but I'le leave him and his parish
to reckon with this cipher.

A Baily or Serjeant.

A SERJEANT is one of the devils tinderboxes, pre-
pared to take and receive the fire of malice into
his clutches, and use it accordingly, tutch and go, touch
and take. Hee's made up of the ruines of poor men,
and rioting of rich ; and all's fish that comes to his
net ; he's the tumbler ; the lercher of a city, corporation, county or shire ; the very puss-cat that watches
the proceedings and creepings abroad of his timerous
mice. Take him simply out of his authority, and he's
a prety piece of impudence ; a kinde of pretender to
some knowledge of the law, as to the practique part ;
and then I cannot wonder at that epitaph upon that
honest lawyer, viz.

God works wonders now and than,
Here lyes a lawyer an honest man.

Since their practice is much like that of the devills,
to go about like roaring lions seeking whom they may
devoure. But alasse, all his knowledge amounts no
farther then petty ignorance ; for he's only skild in the
negative part of the law, viz. you shall never go out of
prison except you pay me my fee 1. His principals, if
he deal with a poor man, are to ly and sweare to lye,
making him believe some strange disasters will befall,
unlesse he compound so and so, or purchase him to be
his friend ; when as he plays Jack of both sides, and
is feed by one side to speak in his behalf to the cre-
ditor, and on the other to terrify and affrighten the
debter ; thus he plays the *hocus pocus* on both sides,
and laughes in his sleve too when he's at home. If he
deals with a rich and crafty knave, then he's at a losse ;
and because he cannot play the knave, he'l be sure to
play the fool, and humour all sides. But he excells
only in his politick art of cunny catching : hee's a notable man to bring about his catchpole designes, for
just like the devil, he deals with every man according
to his temper and inclination.

If he hath the wit to clap up a covetous man, he
enveagles him with the shoeinghorne of a fine bargaine
(and this he doth by a proxie, for fear of distrust) :
and takes him in the way, and carries him to make
the bargaine in the Counter, or prison in stead of the

taverne or alehouses, and then tells him he hath done him a courtesie in saving his money.

If with a friend that he thinks will not mistrust him, he invites him to dinner, and feeds him with a messe of forfeiture, and makes the counter his drawing roome; but for all his art he's sometimes met with, and though he and most of his complices are good lusty pupics, yet they somtimes come short home, and that by weeping crosse. As for your city kestorel, he's never so much puzled as when he's hired to arrest an ins of court gentleman. Then he ventures the infernall pit of a bogg house, and the pilgrim salve of a perfumed dogs turd. Its worth ones sight to see how pittifully he sneaks up and down, for fear the wals should discover his lerching knavery.

But if he chance to light of his pray, oh how he domineers and lords it, and by how much the more he stood in fear, by so much the more he takes upon him. But if once he's catcht as Mosse took his mare, i. e. napping. Then the mercifull gentlemen make him an anabaptist, and fitting it is he should be washt and made clean, who before acted Alderman Atkins. And because they'd have him handsome, he shall be sure have a trimming, though he look, after it, like a calfe halfe lick't. But my subject begins to smell before he comes to his last seasoning; I shall only say, that the whole rout on them may justly be ranked in the number of hell hounds, for their counter is hell, the master of it Belzebub, and the petty foggers his ministring friends, to fetch him in his lively hood.

A Lawyer in Common.

A COMMON lawyer hath been a piece of a scholler in his time; though through his continual use and accustomednesse to break Priscians head and coin new words, he makes no conscience of breaking oaths and men, and of finding new tricks to make a good cause bad, and a bad good. This his trade he learns by degrees; and from petty poverty proceeds to petty villeny and grand knavery. Come to this money-monger without a fee, and he 'le look on you (as the old saying is) as the devill look't over Lincoln, with a squint eye and a bent brow, just as if he was some don of the nation; but pluck but out your chink, oh! then, this melts his heart, and dissolves his tongue into com-plements; now he's your humble servant at least, and he 'le be sure to make you two protestations, but per-form neither, viz. to be faithfull and carefull. And this appears, by his taking of fees on both sides, and so playing the neuter. Thus money is the very soule, the life, the nerves, sinews, muscles and arteries of a lawyer; this is his *forma informans*, it transforms too, for he 'le do or be any thing to every body by virtue of this enchantment: money is the lawyers loadstone, and let him but come within ken of it, and hee 'le do any thing rather than miss his *modicum.* This is one of the politique moles of a commonwealth : and take him out of this his silver clement, and he presently with his brother gives up the ghost and dyes, being deprived of his proper nutriment. This is one of Midas his consanguinity; for though he hath not his fortune, yet he desires it ; and under a pretence of religion, accounts pewter and brasse unsanctified mettle. All these mans wits lies in his fingers ends ; for writing and receiving take up his whole time, except when at the barr, his tongue being before hand oyled with juice of Georges.

But alasse, all trades must live, and ther's an art in every trade, they say : but this is a devilish one I'me sure : to scrue out a fortune out of the ruines of poor men, and pluck them down for self edification. I wonder the good houswives don't purchase these fellows, to spare their candles, for he's an excellent prolonger ; he'l spin a cause out to the very last end, and strives how to continue a suit from generation to generation.

Thus if he finds his circular motives (money, I mean) fluvent. But this beginning to faile, then he begins to lag and laze like a tired jade, and then it must be put to arbitration, I that it must. So that money is the lawyers whip and spur, and they, like rusty ill conditioned jades, woun't go one step without it : thus in

the whole course of a lawyer practice money doth the
feat, and hath a mighty restorative faculty to loose
their tongues, supple their joynts, and to enable them
to say at least your businesse shall be done. These
mens chief employment is in term time; and then,
like so many bees, they are very busie in sucking their
clients. They have no time to think of God nor the
devill then; and observe it when you will, a lawyer
never dyes but in the long vocation; and if death
comes then with a *habeas corpus*, he is so much at
leisure he cannot put in baile to the action : and to
speak truth, I believe the very grief they sustaine by
thinking of so long vacancy and detaineur, from their
spiritus vitalis, money, pines and macerates their
bodys to skelettons and make them degenerate, so as
to be but fit to be Plutos or Minos his under clerkes.

An Informer

IS one of the devils by blows, or rather one of his
lawfully begotten bastards, and he takes right
after his sire ; he play his two parts exactly, which are
to tempt and accuse; if you did but see him sneak
and intrude into gentlemens company, you would conclude him to be some tooth-drawing quacksalver, and
he looks much like those brazen-faced fellows, who go
about to show slight of hand and feats of activity.

His dam was for certain some loose clackt bitch or
other ; and he is so far from being tongue tyed, that he
walks quite cantipodes to the precept here, see and say
nothing. The colloguing gull makes it a piece of his
trade, nay his whole occupation, to provoke and exas-
perate me into some hasty expressions ; and then he
himself, because he would be thought the states bene-
factour, adds to the story, and makes it at least treason
or sequestration ; thus he trapans men into plots, and
then discovers never intended designes ; and though
he himself be the chief and principal agent, yet he
must be the grand witnesse, Signior Swarer.

Thus the blinking polititions of our times, make use
of these stalking asses, these incroaching, dissembling
varlets, that thereby they may hit their marke, the
wigeons and wilde geece of the kingdome. But that
you may beware of this piece of formality, this upstart
shoomaker, or rather tinker, let me give you the markes
of the rogue, and brand his body all over, his hand
hath had it already.

And here I must do as men that climbe up a ladder,
begin at the lower end, and so at last come to the roof
of this thatcht noddle reprobate.

His feet are altogether unclean, he doth not devide
the hoofe, and therefore excommunicate his paths.
Yet he'le dance after every bodies pipe, and turne any
thing, that at last he may catch somthing.

Did you but see him dance (for you must know he

keeps all companies) you'ld sweare he were some weaver; for his legs and his hands go much after the same rate; but he stincks already, his quick motion and speedy vamping from place to place, to gull novices, makes him smell like a traveller; the hogo of the oyle of splayfoot.

But to take a long step, and stride over his ungodly gut, that powdering tub of a gormandizing glutton, that pantry of minc'd meat.

Let us proceed to his breast, neck, hands, and shoulders (for I doubt he'l inform if I stay too long on him). His breast that is much like a haglers panyer, full of rotten eggs, all to be fill'd with the empty shets of foolery, and the rotten yoalks of some stinking underminding enterprices: his neck resembles rather a Jew then a Christian: and his extending his noddle, and straining his crag under some eves, or in some whispering company, to over-hear their discourse, hath brought it to so prodigious a length. His shoulders are of such a latitude, you'ld take him to be a porter; and if you knew him you'd swear he caried his weighty news on his back, but I dare scarce handle his golls, least this pitch defile me, but follow him home, and their you shall see him a writing down all in dismall characters.

But as for his nodle, that sanctified piece of timber (I wonder some great man don't beg it to set it over a paire of great gates), this same matted coxcombe of his is alwaies working, but alas, how many abortive births doth it bring fourth, scarce any take, but candor and clemency are in fault, not his projects : me thinks this sowsing nodle would make a prety good football, it is light and full of winde, shave off but the coblers ends it sow'd with, and it would fly excellent well. I, but what shall we do with his ears if he hath any ? for a hundred to one, if they are not at York and London. Why his reverend ears would serve very well for two leathern patches, to sow to each side his flapt jaws, for this brother hath got too much of the gift of utterance ; and we will stop the mishapen hols widdowed of their flipflops, with pitch and rozen, least there still he retaine also too much of the faculty of enterance. His eys are prety full gogles, dainty rollers ; and he can see plots ; with them see as well as with his ears heare plots. Well, take this monster all together, and hees a clubfooted, hamble shanck't, burstengutted, long-neck't, rattlenodled, large lugg'd eagle ey'd hircocerous, a meere chimera, one of the devils best boys ; but having served him an apprentiship he's now set up for himself, and came out with his wares the last summer *cave tertio.*

A Flatterer.

A FLATTERER is much of the same molde, with the legs and feet of Nebucadnezers immagined image ; part of iron and part of clay, just such another linse-wolsee piece of states policy ; a *hogan mogan* time-server ; he's the meere bolderdash of a commonwealth. Much of the same nature with our late Cromwelist, viz. Carrington, that parsons part of a historian ; that stiles that a compleat history,—which is only the lees of a few conceited actions, setled in the musty caske of his one hogshead nodle, and squeezed into the form of a pamphlet, by the favour of a printing presse.

But to knock out the head of this musty vessell, I'le only say thus much, and so turne him over to the females for a washing tub, viz. that he and his fellows deserve the same fortune that befell that flattering judge, who so farr complying with his incestnous lord, is to tell him, the king might do what he pleased, was at last by the same monarch excorriated and served just as the women in Cheapside do their eeles, and his winding hide hanged over the place of judicature for an example of partiality and flattering.

But to come to my cringing twining willow ; this piece of a panyier makers osiar, O how observant is he in all his joynts to imitate any of the deformed postures of his conceited master, but when he's in any of

his inferiors company, then the stately foole vaunts
and rants his authority in the court; and you had as
good seek gold in the aire, or a needle, as the proverb
is, in a bottle of hay, as extract any courtesy out of
the minerall of his iron breast: but this is one of the
generals that is in the ranck: and he makes it his
whole businesse to informe his majesty of things never
done, and to be sure in any councill, right or wrong,
he'le squeze out arguments, from his spungy nodle, to
second his lords minde, though never so opposite to
right reason. But there are some of a lower ranck;
trencher flatterers, and these hungry villains have so
starved their brains, that they lack wit to do it slyly
and cunningly, I'le leave them therefore in the great
mans kitching, they may serve there to scrape trenchers,
or by their good noses to scent out dinners, and may
perhaps make the man good tarriors and help him to
unkennel the fox. But these dons, of flattery, they
have by the addition of years learned their trade per-
fectly, got just into the nick; and all that they say is
true, now in the flatterers account: they will not stick
to performe the most unworthy action and unbeseem-
ing a man, that they may gain their princes favour: I
could heartily wish that that flatterer of Dionysius,
who licking his spittle from the ground, cryed it was
nectar, might have been forced all his life time to eat
his dung and other excrements, for ambrosia and ne-
penthe. And I can scarce believe but our foremen-

tioned historian, had we but observed him, painted his one nose, and tainted it with a sanguine and copper tincture and complexion, in resemblance of his Mr. firey nostrills. I wonder he did not fall off a coachbox too for company, that so he might the better have described his Mr. patience, in enduring that accident. I can resemble him and the rest of his clawing colloguing brethren to no other then a spanniel, whose fawning eloquence may for a time get them some favour, but their exile commonly is the epilogue, the last act of a tragedy; seldome or never any of them make a commick end. I cannot but averr their motive to this temper and deportment is a cowardly fear of the discovery of their own unfitnesse for state affairs, joyned with a great ambition of being favorites, and these two put together, makes them turne land-water spaniels; all's good that their master doth; their either for duck or partridge. But to conclude, these men are the very vermine of a commonwealth; and all of them so much the more detestable, by how much the more they are known to speak against their own consciences, and against the light of naturall reason.

Of a Temporizer.

IT is storied by St. Jerome in the life of Hikarius, that there was a woman that to every body appeared a beast, to Hilarius only a woman. The same

may be safely averred of this Sr. John Weathercock, he seems to all men a fool, a beast that changes
his coat upon every new spring of alteration in government ; to himself only he seems a politique don :
the only wise man. This puppet of policy differs
from the foregoing spanniel of fawnery only in time
and degrees ; for you shall seldome read of a flatterer
out live his lord : it is well if he hold out so long. But
this politique tumbler skips and hops into diversity of
changing states, and makes that his rule, never to be
so publick for the present state, as to lye liable to be
called in question for it when it changes ; nor never to
be so private and close as to stand neuter in an alteration ; so that he thinks himself the only Jack pudding
of wit, the only juggler in the art of policy. This
polypus changes his colour, and makes it identicall
with the present state under which he lives. If he be
a minister, he'le have a surplice, for the bishop a gowne,
with the modern presbyter a cloak, with an independing Peters. And if times change into popery, he'le
have a cule with the monk. And as the fatt monk
said (when abbeys were a going down, and he obtained
a pension), claping his hand on his belly, *Modo hoc sit
bene,* whats matter for religion, now he had provided
for his gut and rather then stick out, turne shrivers
in nuneries.

If statesmen, then, monarchy, aristocracy, democracy,
are all best all most for the good of a nation. But

whether he be this or the other, it matters not much ;
they agree in their principles, its good to keep in
a whole skin.   These are the true and reall knights of
the post, who swear and forswear, and all in a breath.
If they live under a kingly government, then they can
swallow a covenant with a great deal of formality,
with the right squint and goggle of the eye.   But if
the tyde turns, then they think themselves engaged to
forswear themselves, and turn their former hosanna
into beheading accents.   Now they must dye their
faces with the vermillion blush of an engagement :
and sing with the poet—

    Tempora mutantur, et nos mutamur in illis :

we must follow the mode of the times : as good be out
of the world as out of the fashion.   But your seeking
self-denying, strict walking, hypocritical zealot, he's a
little tainted too with temporizing.   He in the place
fals from the Church into the commonwealth.   And
now he must needs have a division ; but not of
tongues, but of goods.   Then honest Dick sounds as
well as the name of an ell.   But when the wheele of
fortune hath level'd this opinion, they'le rant it in a
worse, if possible : and under a pretence of religion,
turn their Church into a stew : and here also the
rabble follow.   And because they cannot have a com-
munity of goods, they are resolved to have a com-
munity of women.   There Jone's as good as my lady :

and since they can't feast on other mens goods, they are resolved to enjoy their wives. I, but this is just at the last cast; their spoke is just at the ground. And in comes the devill in a quaker; and now we must be all prophets, and prophetesses, and the whole rout follow, but soft, swift. These extasies are onely illusions, chaff of the devils spreading to catch foolish wigeons. These sensorious irrational pieces of mortality inveigh much against the pride of the times, and make humility consist in home-spun attire. Their yea and nay I account as bad as affected swearing, and thee and thou high incivility. But to leave these non intelligent entities, I'le sume up all into the rank of mills. Though some may be turned by the watery scource of discontent, other by the aiery and windy commotions of a brain, and speculative knowledge, and others turned by the hand of strength. Swords must force aw in cowards. Yet all are moved by the main spring of self security and temporary preservation.

A Finnicall London Citizen.

IT is reported of Minerva, or Pallas, that she was begot of Jupiters brain, without the help of a woman. But this compleat crafts master was begot of Midas his cars, by the assistance of a finnicall exchange-woman; and you shall find in him the exact qualities of both his progenitors. His bringing up and education was pretty good, but his greatest perfection consists in the volubility of his tongue, and in the emphatical pronunciation of a What lack you ? His great care in the morning is to get his brazen face into a good *decorum*; and he much admires a handsome prentice, which, as a good sign post and bush in a country town, he thinks draws in customers. He fears much least he should not be trim, and therefore he carries his lookinglasse in his shoes, that so when ever he looks down, he may correct the rumple in his band. And his boy every night rubs and scoures them for the same purpose, least he be the next morning crowned with the heels of them as a pennance for omission. He's a man will scorn to take any affront, and his reason he's a free man. This mans memory is very good in his place, and he runs over his wares with a great deale of celerity. He's no respector of persons ; for, because he'le be in the mode of the times, he Maddames all his customers ; and by his good words cheats the poor gulls, and makes them pay for their high titles. Hee's a man of a very large and spacous conscience, which appears by his large demands, and small receipts ; he'l aske you a pounde for a commodity, and take the third part. And yet by reason of his neatness and trimnesse, he may be said to be a man very exact in his walking. His roses, garters and cuffs putting on, spend the whole morning ; and then with his vineyger cloak, he marches into the shop, and to the Change, with a great deale of gravity, and thinks himself a alderman apparent, at his first setting up. His wife, that trim dame, is his only crosse. For he's forc't to wear out a paire of shoes more in a quarter for her; for he's fane to scrub them half a houre at the doore mat, for fear of fowling the kitching; if he takes tobacco, the sinck is his drawing roome, and he must not spit in her palace, under the penance of a scolding; she's a notable good scold, and will use her tongue, as well as her husband can use his rapier, and better too. This queen, or rather nymph of the queene of faries, is a very costly dame, and must eat nothing but dainties and dear bought cates, dressed in ample manner, which makes them both very often to fall from high faire, and rich clothes, to the counter, and the brokers. Did you but see her husband and she, with what devotion they walk to Isllington cake-house, you would think them some zealous sacrificers in there ceremonicall works. Every May she goes to hear the cucko sing, but that is the only sorrow of her husbands zealous braine. They are the only wise ones in the city; but in the country, the only fools and ignoramouses. The only notable and gallant day is on that day they call my Lord Mayors day, and then my gallant squires of the cloth are in all their *pontificalibus*. If he's a young man, he's whifler to the company, which is much of the same nature with a dog whiper; and then he marches

with his white rod and golden chaine before his company; if he comes to the honour of a gowne, you'd
take him to be a hog in armour, just such another
bumble arst furfact piece of mortality. But when he
comes to be master of a company, or alderman or
lord mayor, then he's at the height of his preferment,
and he must take on him by his place. And then he,
who before was good at light waits, short yards, scant
measure, is the only best man to discover his own fore-
past knaveries; there I leave him to order his upstorts
in the art of knavery.

A Hide-Parke Lady.

IT is fabled of Orion, the son of Hirius, that he was
begote by the urin of Jupiter, Mercury, and Nept,
when they pissed in the ox hide, with the flesh of
which these three gods were feasted by Hircus, but
how likely this is, judge you. Yet we may justly
think these salacious females to be of such another extract, as being the wanton kidds of their old insatiate
goatfathers. But its but a folly to pry into their *ma-
toria prima*, because a good father may generate a bad
child, and a bad father as good one. But look on them
as they come hurrying with their horses and rattling
with their chariots to the gale of this aiery place, you
could not but mistake them for vapors by their light

carriage. There is some marks, and they but a few, left of the image of God in their faces ; for the rest are covered with the shreds of the devils mantle (I mean those) black spots and patches of deformity, and now their leaporde skin is freckled with the marks of the beast, and markt with the devils insignes.

I cannot but wonder these shavings of the brokers trumpery should be so much in fashion now in these bad times, unlesse it is to shew humility, by an ante-penstasis, or to mock God by blazoning our faces with sables, and have in our hearts our ox. But to passe by these marks of a Jesabell, look on her cariage and deportment, and you shall finde her a Lucifer in the abstract, a prety kinde of a gawdy peacock, folowed by a proud turkey-cock. Thus she and her brusling gallant, whose whole erudition lyes in the formall pronunciation of madam and such finickle accents, and in swearing in print, and as they call it *ad unguem*, with a specious flattery of her ladiships eye, nose, cheek, hand, body, &c., make one of the many puppes that are in the play. Their whole imployments is to gaze and look to see how the wanton beauties of our age, like the wheele of fortune, run round the ring. And there, as it is reported between Cæsar and Pompey, that one could not abide a superior, the other an equall ; so these fenes of finery quite undoe the grammarian, by quite extinguishing the degree which is called superlative. And thus they spend their malice and envy,

I

each faulting the others face and gesture, and thinking
her self the only master piece of the pack.

Καὶ γὰρ ἐπὶ γλάιες ζηλέμονες ἐισι γύναικες.

Then after these lustfull platonnicks have had a sufficient contemplation of each others ideas, for I cannot
give a more substantial expression to such a violatile
subject, a way march they by paires, or perhaps they
have by this time increast their company, and having
glutted their eyes, now they must pamper their ungodly guts, and lustfull cates are held onely expedient
for lustful employments ; and the cup, the platter, and
a coranto take up the time till midnight, and then to
kennel march my hounds, and to hogsty my swine.

But this little magpy of chattering eloquence never
uses her judgment, in censuring and condemning so
much, as when her finified cracklowse brings home her
to'ther gowns : now her eagle eyes spie out the least
unmannerly misdemeanour of her upstart courtier ;
and because her joy and delight is in a ternacy number,
it must march at least thrice to the botchers for trans-
mogrification, though her nimble shankt nipshred never
medles with the garments : and so deceives his Argus
ey'd madam. Her mornings are spent in trimming
and decking her unsanctified corps ; and she surely
concludes her patience to be superabundant, and much
in imitation to that of Jobes, because she can endure
to be so long in dresing. Take her altogether, shee's a

meere whirlegig, a piece of painted clay layd over with the watry colours of red and white, which when the streaks of old age have a little scarified, she fills up with a supliment of untempered mortar, and thinks to mend and repaire the decay'd morter of her face with the artificiall clay of a painting Jesabell. Take her altogether, and she's in generall the jay of the age; in particular, she's crowned with a right womans wit, thats none at all; her face represents the signe of the checker, her naked breasts the flesh pots of Egypt deckt with a seeming comlinesse her body, the stew of an Italian corporation, and her whole self the common Hide-Parke lady, that is, if unmarid, one that longs for a husband, and for want makes use of her little lacque; if wedded, one that picks up stalions as a begger doth chips in a frosty morning, to supply present necessity and the dificiancy of conjugall fuell.

The Good old Cause.

THIS bad new cause may justly be compared to the rhetorick of a nonsensicall mountebank, which he uses to signifie, not what he means, or what he can doe; onely they are intended to pussel poore mens intellects, and catch their fancies into an admiration, to the loosing of their money; just such a painted flag of policy is this, whose end is to allure us to close with it, and under a specious pretence of I cannot tell what platonical immaginary felicity, to wheele us, and egg us into an abysse of slavery : this is that politique mous-trap, baited with the moldy cheese of formall pretences, which at last will dwindle and decline into an apparent fallacy, and bring upon us a dilemmaticall confusion. And the devil useth the same art in moral policy, as he hath done in spiritual ; endeavouring to cover over the lurcking blasphemies of an upstart heresie with famous pretences, and paint them over with the sucus and tincture of whorish and Jesabell expressions, thinking by the suggercandy of expression to make the soule damning tenents go down more glibbery : such are these. An evangelical hunnycombe, a new light, a gospell revelation, and spiritual perfection. Thus I say in morall policy, he hath gotten a bait to catch the gaping and greedy men after innovation, deluding them by verball expressions.

Thus, like an occæcated Tobit, do the purblinde polititians of our tottering common-wealth send forth before them this dog, this their fawning dog of faire seeming pretences, to make them way to those preferments, which like egs at Grand Cario, are all ready hatched in the ovens of their hot and fiery pericranium's. But still this good old cause lacks searching, and requires a finer probe of wit to dive into, than the dull and dismall phansie of my illiterate intellect is able to afford. But a little to illustrate it, we must consider the several kindes of causes, and see to which of these, or whether to all these, this good old cause is a retainer. A cause, then, is either *efficiens, materialis, formalis principalis, minus principalis, finialis.* For I shall not stand to an exact logickal division and subdivision.

If they by this good old cause mean *causa efficiens,* then it is that usurping cause or principall which inheres in the phantastique braine of an unsetled trouper, whereby he endeavors to stettle himself in such a ruling decorum, as to effect and produce his own weale and safety, sink or swim common weal, and spirituall and ecclesiastical weal together.

This now may be called an old cause, because it hath its product from self-seeking, that branch of original corruption ; but how it may be called good, I know not, unlesse it is *respectu seipsorum ;* and that is so farr from good in a ruler, to minde only private occasions, that heathens have condemned it for unsufferable.

If you take it for *causa materialis,* then you must annex that substantive ruine to it ; for where the cause and means be bad and impious, the effect must needs be matter of ruine and impiety. As to the materiallity of this cause, the *materia prima* must needs be like that in the braines of an Aristotle, empty and aiery notional, and phantasticall ; for the first matter springs from a timpany of conceited greatnesse, and an overweaning phancy of deserving and meriting ;

by the biting of this brye they run headlong after superiority, under the notion of a good old cause.

As to the *materia secunda,* the second matter of this cause, will be matter of mourning and lamentation to England (if it proceed) in respect of us; of tyranny and irreligion, and multiplicity of herecies in respect of them. Thus the materiall cause is but pride and hypocrisy, self conceitednesse and vain-glory, which, when it once comes to get the upper hand and rule, never goes without the company of its second and companion: viz., cruelty and irreligion, schismaticall heresies and profanenesse; if you consider it as *causa formalis,* a formall cause, why then you consider it just as it is; for it pretends faire, and professeth a Herods delight in the John Baptists of our time, I mean the godly ministers; but intendeth nothing lesse then their supporture, nothing more then monarchicall tyrany and usurpation. Just like the devill in Samuels mantle, and like our Saviours comparison of the tombs, an outside Saint lin'd with the devill within, outward promising, inward treason.

Thus they set a formal and hypocriticall face, and a formall and deceiving cause; like to like, quoth the devill to the colier. Consider it as *causa principalis,* and *minus principalis.* For I am almost a weary of this causelesse cause, and it will prove the principall, chief, and most notorious cause of innovation and traitorisme, the lesse principall cause of all mutuall divisions, distractions, unsettlement and quarells. The principall cause of quakerisme, papisme, anabaptisme, fifth monacrisme, and also striving for superiority, to the undoing our commonwealth; and thus it may be called the devills old cause of heart burnings, envies, malice, and cut-throating. Thus *causa causæ est causa causati*. Take it as *causa propinqua* and *remota*, and so in brief the devil's the remote cause, and their hearts the approximate and neere propinque cause of this dissenting cause. The truth is, the only cause they seek is matter of warr and dissention ; the provocking cause is their accustomednesse to live idle and keep hy company, and the remote cause their want of money (which is remote from them), to maintaine this idle life and ranting company ; and to speak aright, it would be hard for the tinker to return to his snap-sack, the cobler to his all, the weaver to his shuttle, or the brewer to his dray ; and, therefore, they are resolved, before they will do it, tinker wise, to make two holes in a devided commonwealth ; in mending one, to stitch up their consciences with the coblers-end of resolvednesse in sin, and chock and stifle it in the graintub of resistance, before they'l returne, as they call it, with the dog to their vomit, and the sow to her wallowing in the mire. But if you look on it as *causa finalis*, the finall cause, its end may prove misery and affliction to us, but surely without repentance damnable to them ; but, however, this is not the end of the cause, but the end of the caused effect of the cause. Therefore, this good old cause hath a two fold end, as they call it ; one in respect of it self, and thats self advancement, and monarchy ; the other in respect of others, and that is debilitating and oppression of opposites, advancing and approving complices, and heretiques ; but take this cause together, and it is a mad piece of pedling policy, and no more to be maintained, or mentioned by a rationall man, that pretends to wisdome, then sensuality ; it is a fantastique, whinesicall, ruinous self-seeking hipocriticall, irreligious, contentious and destructively ruinous cause, whose pretences, though never so faire, will be found not only to come short of that good they pretend, but include all pernicious evill to be immagined. But we must pray that this cause may never come to effect.

A detracting Emperick.

AN emperick is one whose chief excellency consists in hard words and sentences, and in a fine bombastique oratory, accompanied with detraction from the credit of his betters, and commendation of his own farr fetcht experience. His first originall is from a poor apothecaries' subservant, whose work is to look to the stills and sweep the shop, who, having got a smatch and relish of their nonsensicall gibberish, and stolen

some of his masters receipts, at the end of his time
makes an end of his master, and the next market day
sets up for himself; his first adventures are upon the
swetty toes and butter teeth of country jobsons, whos
hard travel and dry crusts make their grinders and
carriers in an unserviceable condition. After, his impudence encreasing, not his wit, then out he comes in
half a sheet a paper, a French doctor; and his pitifull
retainers plaister him on every post and wall, with a
lying account of his exquisite parts and great skill.
And these are the men that attest he hath wrought
wonders on their bodies; but, however, lets give you a
glimps of his profession. This excrement of an apo-
thecary, this quackroyall is never so much himself, as
when he's a pratling on things he cannot understand,
and never so happy as when he's a puzling the dull
intellects of his silly patients with Greek, Latine words,
and telling them what fractions, disloetions he hath set,
how many humours he hath asswaged by frication,
how many megrimicall and hypocondriacal humors he
hath dissipated, what marvelous unheard of cures he
hath done in places where he never was, nor ever will
be; and then to all his brags he cannot passe by the
mentioning of the weakness and unsufficiency of other
doctors, and what a want of experience there is in
most of them, for want of his travels. Thus this
politique glisterpipe runs himself into a kinde of small
practice for a time, but they all learn his simplicity at

K

last, which vexes him to the guts. For like the kite, who, having over-laid her maw with carrion, and vomiting it up, thought she had parted with her guts ; so this scum of a closestool thinks himself ruined by their departure. But, however, because he will be a right traveller indeed, and so may lye by authority, he never stays in a place above a fortnight, but makes himself an *individuum vagum*, under pretence of the common good, and because he will not hide his tallent in a napkin, his candle under a bushel. But if he had his due, he should have a paire of stocks at least ; for the grave is his friend in receiving those he murders. This is the man who is the lord paramount of all doctors, and dares try it out with Gallen or Hipocrates, but shewes never so good sport as when two of them meet together in a market. Then like two mastiffs they fall on for the prey, and by this means the people escape a cheating. Then these quacks peale out each others weaknesse ; and because they know each others weaknesse, and because they know their own originalls, they discover their own knavery to the bottome. But their greatest skill lies in the French pox. How coms that about ? Only by self experience ; for such idle vagabonds lay themselves open to all such impious suggestions. But let not me tire my self with these *hocus pocusses* of doctorisme, but leave them to their ignorance, to scrape a living out of their equalls.

A Colledge Butler.

A COLLEDGE buttler is much of kin to those worms who take up their habitations in learned volumes, who overrun whole pages to their little emolument; even thus this finicall attendant spins out his time amongst the learned, and lives amongst a succeeding stock of phylosophers, and yet remains as meer an animal as the former, no whit a proficient, but inferiour to his emblem; for it dyes it self over with a blushing tincture, as being ashamed of its own negligence; but this calves skin impudence brazens it out with a cuckolds-face; and what he lacks in reality, he supplyes in shew and affectation. This spicket of a university man is much accoutred with complements, and is able in the country to quite astonish an honest farmer, and when he travels, goes at least for a justice of the quorum. Nay, this presumptious chip crust thinks himself to be at present of kin to the lawyers (and hopes all others do so too), and doubts not but to be a judge in time, since he already gets his living by sizes. And could this tapdropping but unmask and unveile the knaveries of the state or church, so well as he can excoriate a loafe, and bring down the lofty tumors of its swelling pericranium, he would prove an unmatchable piece of sliving policy, and the onely man fit for a protectorship: but it is to be feared, if once

this man should soare into any place of credit, he
would soon become hereticall and dangerous, for he
hath been continually exercised in, and hath his living
by schismes and divisions : and indeed he may claime
some kin to the former sophoi of literature, for he
divides and subdivides with much sharpenesse.   He is
a good anatomist to scrue into the very center of a
loaf, and to pry into the joynt of separation.   A good
surveyour only, he measures not by the chaine nor the
quadrant, no, by the retundant rather, i. e. the jugg.
I shall not insist much of his dealing with Bellarmine,
that is known to every fresh man, but only take notice
of his equall and unpartiall justice in his distributions,
which is so exquisite and plausable, that he thinks him
self another Aristides, not a scruple doth he give to
one more then another.

An excelent arethmetitian he is, and most accurate
in accounts ; he's blameable in nothing but in that he
will be sure to charge the schollers noddles, which
should be fraught with learning, with the strange and
unwelcome letters of ob, and in so much that these
strange and unknown characters make freshmen take
him for a necromancer.   But did you but see him
dominere over a freshman, you'd soon conclude him to
be some extraordinary officer, when as, poore caitiff,
when they come to be sophs, the pump is his reward
for his insolencies.   But to come to his office, he's so
used to spread cloaths, that he's ne're well but when

he's unspreading of aprons, and spreading of females sails, in so much that he often comes to be a father, before he's either willing or provided. He keeps all things in order but himself, for the continuall use of mault-juice, which he powres down continually, makes him alwayes dizzey.

His tables are alwayes full of Latine characters, which makes the country-man think him an excellent schollar at his first coming, but staying a while, he hath much a doe to think of his home, for his head poizes his whole body ; his exact accounts will not let a quart passe unaccounted, which if it chances to remain an odd one, he'le be sure to make it up, because he'le have an even quantum. If any thing kills him, it will be a grief, because under graduates are stinted, who are the fresh drinkers, and love to his own gain makes him give them a little liberty to exceed. But to take away this university man, and to fold him quite up by giving him his due, you may broach him an exquisite gut servant, who's own belly is his best clock, which though it onely gives warning at 8. 11. 3. 6. 8. yet is sure to be exact then to a punctilio. This the cook and the bed maker are the Cerberus of a colledge, if you take them under a general notion ; but divide them accurately, and they are the necessary evils of an accademian. The cook he's the grasier, the poulterer and fish-monger of the society ; the bed-maker must be ranged amongst the huntsmen, because

of their kennels ; and the butler, he's the whiffler to go
before and prepare for the cook, and the lievtenant to
bring up the reere, and place things as they were : but
I shall doe by him as he by a loaf, martyr him into too
many subdivisions. I shall therefore leave him lockt
up in his binn.

A Vniversity Beadle.

THIS is the arse gut of an accademy, the meere
lacky of a vice-chancellor in a black gown and a
round cap, much of kin to those hinch-boys, who on
my lord mayors day at London, were wont to run
before my lady marice in velvet caps, &c. But to give
him his due, he hath been a schollar in his time, and
fellow perhaps of a colledge, but as they say, when
drinks in wits out, so when the bellygod hath been a
feast-hunting, the vapours of his stomach clowd the
light and hinder the infuence of his cerebrum if he
hath any. This man by his place is the prologue of
the vicechan., and every exercising master of arts. His
chiefest imployment is in gathering congregations, and
giving notice of clerums, which if it be in morning or
afternoon he doth plenore : I can compare him to none
more aptly then Milo, who by continuall using to carry
a calf at lest could bear an ox : even so this officer, by
continuall feasting his gut, and indulging his paunch,

he's come to so great a proficiency in the art of gluttony, that it is not oxen will serve his turne. His senting haires are still quick and tender, and he hath as thinne a nose as any dog in the pack ; if he walks he'l smell a feast as far as Trumpinton or Coton, and foot it accordingly, hunting dry foot with extream celerity and labour, till he hath obtained his prey, and then a game at noddy disgests all. He's cousen-germain to the fatt monk, who hearing that abbies should go down, got a pention, and then clapping his hands on his ungodly panch, said, *Modo hoc sit bene*, if this thrive but, alls well ; so this *Marriotus redevivos renatusq.* makes his *venter* the *primum mobile* of all his actions, that makes them in stature to be so like to the Anakims and Zansummims.

It may be said of him as it was of Bonosus, that rebelled against M. Aurel. Valer. Probus, that he was borne *non ut viveret sed aut biberet :* so of this he was borne *non ut viveret sed ut ederet :* for as other men only eat that they may live, so this only lives that he may eat, and if once university revenues should be taken away, either you'd soon hear of his death of a consumption, or else you'ld hear of his metamorphosis into an anthropophagus. Never till I was at Cambridge did I see the logicians chimæra, his Hircocrervus, but when I had a view of it in a beadle, he's a Hircus in his wanton endeavours after dainties, and a Cervus in his speed and festination he maks to obtain

them, his fear of loosing, and his quick hearing the
rumor of them. And I much wonder he hath not long
since been carried and shown at Bartholmew faire for
a sight.

His first place, or his ushering in of the actors makes
him seem a retainer to a stageplayer, though he is
swelled up with a timpany of pride in conceit of his
fine office ; did you but see him delivering his verses
he understands not in his coife, you'd take him for
some bearded London coster-wife newly drest up on a
munday morning. But to make an end with him, he's
the *materia prima* of a *tripus* or *prævericator*, the
very *causa sine qua non*, of all his quibles, and one
that is fit for nothing else but to be made the fool at a
commencement vacation. Should I run through the
organs of this accademick body and the favorites of
independing presbyterianisme, would put him down
and bruise his pipes, being angry with the harsh me-
lody of such a tincklering instrument. I shall therefore rather leave the filling of his stuft parts to the
bellowes of a more strong invention, having wearied
my self already with so fulsome a subject.

A Covetueus Usurer.

A COVETUOUS usurer is cousen german to good
Monsieur Midas ; and though perhaps his fools
noddle is not furnished with so good a pair of asses

cars, yet he could wish his fingers might have a little of the same virtue. Take him in a morning, and his worships spectacles adorn his nose, and direct and guide his industrious pen in arithmetique, and debts, and mortgages are all viewed over once a day, which is his breakfast ; for the miser accounts that amongst the number of *innecessaria.* Take him about noon, and his stomach is a preparing for his dinner by a walk : and then this threadbare companion lookes much like a broken citizen, that cannot afford himself a new suit ; but to be short, his purse and his gut take up all his time, but chiefly his purse ; his yellow and white blessings are so much in his thoughts, that his onely care is to live and encrease his money and dye, and there is an end. But as shottenly as he looks, he's a notable crafty fox in his way, and will make a bargain with any man in England. Oh how he pin'd and murmur'd when it was brought to six in the hundred ; that fit of sicknesse had almost brought him to the grave. His greatest delight and complacency is in the acquaintaince with young spend-thrifts : these he loves for their papers sake ; oh he'd fain be fingering there, and to be sure not a farthing will he lend till he hath twice the value in land made over to him ; and then he hugs and blesseth himself, and never gives over reading, and hopes there will never come a redemption. These are his onely delight, and though he hates, yet he loves their extravagancies ; did you

L

but know in what fear he is, when any of his gods lye
dormant, and how he crowds them together, and
watches his trunk, and locks his chests, and bars his
hutches, you'ld think, nay conclude, his life, his very
animal spirits, were contained in his coffers. Thus this
miserable earthgrubber doth not onely acquire this
trash with vexation and labour, envy and malice, but
is perplexed, distracted, distrustfull to keep it also. If
he be a batchelour, he's the more happy man ; for the
very charge of a wife and barnes, would (as they say)
put him out of his seven senses. His diet now is
onely what mice and rats will not eat, moldy bread
and old cheese. For, quoth Mr. Provident, is it not a
sin to let such vermin destroy the good creature ? but
his minde is in his counting-house ; did you but take
a strict account of that Fryday face of his, whose
rowsey whiskers and brischy turn-pikes make him
resemble some shaggy meteor, or some borish Turk,
you could not but smile and burst your spleen with
laughing, to think what a dish of butter'd crablice his
mossy excrement contains fat and in good liking. I
wonder he sels not his head to some ale wife, it would
make an excellent Sarazen signe, if he could but spare
it. His rinckled jaws, like an old cows neck, hang
chathernwise, lank and loose ; his whining and pelting
posture have distracted his chops beyond their bounds,
and his skin to a greater and more large extention, so
that now it superabounds in vacuits, and like his grand

sires double ruff hangs in pleats and folds, his eyes
are dim'd before he's thirty ; for he hates candles, and
pores in the dark if his arithmatical occasions require
speed. I wonder he gets not a glow-worm to save
charges ; his band (of his own patching) becomes him
very well, and suits the other habliments of his body ;
and for brevity sake, to save soape, cloth, water, and
time, is not extended beyond the dimensions of his
collar ; and for another reason, if necessity force him,
a clean shirt may supply both offices.

His hands and his gloves alwaies goe together, he
hates artificiall ones, because they are apt to weare out
and seam rend. His doublet and breeks are of the
oldest fashion, for he keeps a Jewish jubile, and he
never gives rest to his cloaths but once in 7. years, and
that never to serve him more ; he's such a constant
man, he hates mutation. Thus you may know a
usuring bachelour by his mode, which is out of mode.
If he hath got a wife, oh poor woman, she'd better be
hanged ; for exclamations against expences and charges
are never out of his mouth. O what afflictions doth
he meet with each moment, a peniworth of butter, a
halfpenyworth of salt, two peny worth of milk, soap
and candles, to pay for fire and meat, house rent and
cloath, oh, oh, oh, enough to undoe a poor house-
keeper. Well, he's a house keeper now, and the
colectors for the poor give him daily visits ; often he's
abroad, though alwayes at home, and he payes these

just as his brother batchelour, if he have lands, pays
taxes after a long conflict. When at home, with what
deliberation doth he pull forth his greasy powch, and
accompany its production with a sith; then the un-
willing hand he forces to dive into and search for
his heart blood, which is accompanied out with a
hideous groane; but when its gone, he thinks he's
bound by naturall affection to give it a parting showre
of tears, though the losse of a wife would not come half
so near him. And she's like to suffer for all, and eat
nothing but flotten milk this fortnight, for this trick.

Thus this money bag, like a hide bound horse, never
evacuates any of his mettle, but with sorrow and
regreate, me thinks a purge might do well; plurasies
are very dangerous, a little phlebotomy's good physick.
But this retentive faculty of his, he thinks is his great
vertue. Provide for thy family is his proof; nay,
rather than heel be an infidel in not getting, heel be so
in not trusting his nearest friends without a mortgage,
and his poorest without a pawn. And thus he builds
and lays *Pelion* upon *Ossa*, one bagg on another, till
death trips up his heels, and his young son pulls them
down. Thus this muck worme never leaves delving
till a damp over takes him and puts out this candles
end. Oh how it delights him (when he's past hark-
ning after chapmen, and past seeking after spenders),
to hear frugality, as he calls it, commended, and prodi-
gality laid out in its proper colours, when alasse he's

far from the golden mean, *incidit in Sylam dum vult vitare Carybden,* just in the extreame. Well, to put a period to my coffer keeper, follow him in all his plots and proceedings, and you'l find him just like a horse in a mill, that though he uses continuall motion, is still where he was ; even so this man, for all his pains and getings, is as miserable, nay more then the most indigent, and is never the better, he lives never the more comfortably, does never the more good for all his riches.

A Cambridge Minion.

A CAMBRIDGE parakeeto is an outlandish ape, whose mimick disposition makes her shape her seacole vestures into the form of the fashion ; though her self be quite out of shape, a meere petty chaos of dust and ashes ; half animated and lickt over by the flattering tongue of some puny freshman : she's one of the times beauties in her own conceit, and though her fingers are shriveled with exercising a landresses function throughout the week, yet on Sunday she bridles it according to her own imagination ; and with don Quiro orecomes all the stout sophs of her diocesse, by the strength of her own fancyed beautifull perfections. Her Sundays imployment after evening prayer is a walke, and that day she accounts to be a market one, for then she displays the soiled ware of her pedling face to the view and sail of all in its most artificiall decking. Thus have I read of a garulous crow bedecking it self with the gawdy plumes of a supercillious peacock; and an emblematicall ass sprucefyed with the gorgeous trappings of a lofty beusephalus : and thus this sweeping of a schollars bed-chamber invelops her course gran'd hide in vestures of a madam, and though, poor soul, she starves within dores and pinches for't all the year after, her gown and other accoutrements shall extend beyond the *ne ultra* of her ability. But she becomes them accordingly, and they hang about her fusty corps, much after the rate as if hang'd on with pitch-forks, so that she is finely slutish, and sluttishly fine; I wonder what she would do with her yellow golls, were it not for her apron and stomacher; for they are the only upholders of those masy quarters, squeesed into the narrow compasse of a finicle paire of gloves, to the danger of overheating her foggy flesh; and when all is done, rowling pin like, it seems to be a confused lumpe of flesh, not a hand, its more like a foot. Her squint eyes are for the most part fixed on the ground, neither dares she lift up her gogles for fear of prejudicing her chast modesty : but yet an occult leere is now and then cast at a transient schollar. Her swimming and frigging gate denotes something of levity, though her set countenance proclaimes a *noli me tangere.*

Take her upon the account of an husband, she's a notable, quaint, precise, curious, wary and cautious dame ; she looks high ; a gentleman schollar is her scope, her marke ; her fellow townesmen she scornes, as being below her merrit : oh, she affects courtship extreamly, and loves above all things to be saluted with a madam-eticall title ; she curtesies in print, observing both mood and figure, and can if need be sing you a merry song and be pretty joculatory : and though in town or before company she's something coy and occultly reserved, yet in *private* she is as free of her flesh as an emperor, and will afford her company a whole night at any time, provided you prepare good store of cates for her licquorish chops, and wine too, for she loves to make use of the creature. She hath a notable politique way of begging, by an exclamation of her wants, and she'le ware her worst gloves on purpose that she may by finding fault purchase new ones.

If she be any thing handsome, she knows it too well ; and if any sort of portion or pedigree she can claime too, then she soares high ; pentioners and undergraduates are of too mean a stock, to low and unworthy, to pretend service to her : no, because shee's a gawdy fool her self, she'le be sure to chuse her fellow, her like a gentleman fellow commoner, to be sure or a master of arts, that gos in his fine half shirts : these she seeks to enchant by her devotion at church ; and these most of them have more wit then to be what they seem, only kisse her and feel her a litle, and leave her to the next.

Take them all together, and they all of them appear to me to be of the same extraction, and originall with Venus, begot of the froth of the sea, or rather by some frothy or light timbred fellow commoner, that makes them so gravely light and fantastical. But to give you the taile, marke and brand of this fine whimsicall piece of scholarship, you may know her by these ensuing characters.

First, by her Bartholmew face, her affinity in pole trimming with the plays of that toy faire; if she be of any mean extraction, her flying coifes intimate her soaring intentions, and she looks in those starcht conundrums like a little meat mins't and slice't and laid in order, in a prodigiously great charger. Neither will her whitewine and wild tansy burnish over her rusty brazen face, so as to bring it to a right posture; but she'le be sure, because she'l be gay, to wear in her visage the right Bartholomew fools coulers, red and yelow. The continuall bleaching and whitening her Mr. Schollars linnen, makes her wollen face of a tallow complection, jumping with the proverbe,

> March winde and May sun
> Makes cloths white, but maidens dun.

But, perhaps, the brewers daughter of our colledge will be angry; she'le make our bear so small for this, it

shall never smile on us more. Nay, pray Mis. Ale-
berry, sweet Mis. Graine tub, hunny Mis. Copper face,
be not to angry. I hope you do not think I intend to
spoil the use of your mashing fat by these lines, or
have a designe to make your skipping suiters hop away
and leave you : no truly, I wish you so good a brewer
to your husband, as may carry about him such effec-
tuall barm, as may set the musty hogshead of your
pawnch a rising and swelling, to the production of a
Bacchus, a better man then his father ; but don't mistake me, I don't wish you Semeles fortune, viz. to be
imbraced by your clarke underneath your copper in
the midst of his searching thunderbolts. No indeed
forsooth, if you'l believe me forsooth, I don't forsooth ;
only forsooth a good lusty malthorse forsooth, your
husband forsooth, thats all forsooth.

These petty ladies whose fathers have obtained them
a kind of a petty fortune, are of anothers guesse hue
then the former ; for their countenances are bedizned
in sable sacks, or it may be in white sarcenet wallats,
which alwaies intimates their husbands fortune.

If dame nature hath been riged as to deny them
red and white, they can buy some, and so plaster accordingly ; but though they think to hide their snouts
over with size and whiting, all will not do ; you may
know them by the cast of the ey, the purse of the
mouth, and the coy cariage of their weighty nodle,
whose trembling motion and wagging posture denotes

M

something, but thus much for the face, I fear I have painted them too right.

Secondly, know her (because I have spent too much paper on her) by the rest of her body and gate. Her breasts you shall be sure to know by their affinity with the udder of our sandy cow and your brown heifer, which she lays open as she thinks for temptation sake, but alas, these her milk-pails lack a little scouring; she must serve them as good housewifes do theirs, bestow a little sand and straw on them, or they will nere be oughts. Her gant belly and her bushel arse denotes her a maid; but her wanton eye and affected gate show it is much to her affliction : but her crupper arse is to be sure beautified with a gawdy traping ; I wonder she don't hang bells at them, she'd make an excellent forehorse. Take her altogether, and she's a fine finacle Cambridge production, got by and aiming no higher then some suckspicket sophister.

A Pune Pragmatick Pulpit-filler.

HE is one that can say to corruption, thou art my father : for the corruption of his manners at the university generated the odium of the master and fellows to such a height, that they had brought forth the birth of expulsion, if he by this preventing medicine of giving them a vale (as one wittily saith) *nihil*

ante dictum, had not cashecred himself their jurisdiction. And we all know the rediest way for such is to
get a pulpet and teach others what they scarce understand ; nay, cannot maintain by syllogisticall dispute
themselves. So that I may justly describe him to be
a half stewed codling'd philosopher, a linsewoolsy
logitian, &c. and with illustrious Cleaveland, call him a
lay interlining clergyman. And me thinks these John
Lacklatines creep into benefices, like foxes into hen-
rousts, only to fill their empty guts (starved as much
for want of food, as their noetical faculties devoid of
all philosophick irradiations, and as their *perecranium*
dark and gloomy, dismall and obscure, for want of the
gilding and glistering rayes of the sun of good erudition) : and to supply the vanities of their elbowes, I
mean their froward and fretfull doublets, whose continuall and quotidian vexations by rubs and foiles, hath
quite worne out the patience of the nap, and the long
suffering of both warp and woolf. And, like their
brother reynard, though their intention be onely their
own emolument, yet they keep out and hinder their
betters, and spoile and mangle the good food of the
word (just as old women their naturall meat with the
blunt and notcht cuttles of their wit). T'would grieve
your heart to hear what work these sand drope makers
make with an easy and facile text, into what far fetcht
notions they dissolve it, and how miserably they are
forced to wander from their businesse, to patch up

their piece of stuff to the length of the houre glasse.
And yet this apothegmaticall licosthenes will bring
you up whole legions of examples, and quote you those
authors he never saw, much lesse read : and his Greek
and Latine spouts from his originall jaws as water from
a cesterne redundant with that element. And thus this
new consecrated Levite gets the aërial and vaine applause of the vulgar, who cryes him up for a great
losopher and an excellent scholarde ; nay, I warrant
you, they take him at least for a conjurer. And truly
the brazen faces and nimble clacks of these, by the
help of that smatch of divinity they have, may serve
for edification and be good, but there are another sort,
who as they have neither wit of their own, nor fancy
others, but fill up their sermon with the riff raff of
their own nodles, and a heaped congeries of imperti-
nent and inapposite Scriptures, and a multitude of
illogicall acatagoricall reasons and arguments : these
are they that hammer out a sermon, like an unknown
unwonted unseen oration ; and because their time shal
be spent at church, their clumsy fists and squint eys
will be sure to have half an hours busling at every
proof, before the hold-my-staffe can finde it ; for as
the proverbe saith, it is to him as bad as seeking a
needle in a bottle of hay. His studies are as small as
his brains, for its one of the torments of his life to
think of his Sunday employment, and that makes him
a speciall friend to the booksellers, old obsolete and

Noahcall sermons, and these are the parchments he especially takes care of it. But it may be objected here by the clown his father, nay, I cant believe this, sir : for my son must needs be a good scholard, for he's seldome without a book in his hand, and I'me sure he can speak good Latine. I answer, sir, for your comfort, your son is a tolerable thunderbolt ; an indifferent good Hanctulo, for to be sure, though he reads but little, yet his parts are so ripe, and he's so exquisitely gifted, that though he reads but little, yet whatever it is, he makes it his own. But a querie now arises among the Quakers, whether this be not petty felony to rob the dead and the quick ; and what religion this is to offer up that in the temple that costs them nought. Truly, friend, for answer you shall have nothing but the old proverbe, I would they were hang'd that want one shift ; I would he was hanged has one too many. But to conclude with the time, I should be very sorry if I should overtire your patience with any inconvenient language or prejudiciall sentences in this character ; it is not the function but abuse of it I condemn ; the former I reverence and love ; this latter proceeds from a timpany of pride inherent in the platonicall pericranium of an empty nodled sophister, or from the dropsicall humors of a young suckspiting junior, whose manners being remora's to his studys and degrees, have forced him to take the wings of an owle, and flying forth, he thinks to enlighten others with his

own dim and gloworm understanding to the prejudice
of the function, which is much scandald by such empty
novices, whose empty nodls seek nothing but to be
filled with the vaine breath of applause, though all
their conundrums and bombastic pettifoging deserves
rather a satyr then a panegirick.

An old Hording Hagg.

SHE is one of the Wich of Endors cosen-germans,
that for a little yellow dirt or white clay will
court the devill himself in a Samuels mantle, nay pro-
strate her body and soul to the devotion of idolatrizing
Mamon ; she's a woman of a notorious faith ; it hath
in it all dimentions, longitude, latitude, and prefundity.
Her money is her god, and shes an implicite papist.
The reason why she scrapes her copper quarter peny
coyn into her fusty pouch, made of the last sheding of
the lanck and loose skin of her hoary buttock (for she
therein immitates deere) till it amounts to the sacred
number of 6. score (for her hundred is of the largest
size) is because she is a saint worshiper, and loves to
pray to the image of St. George in a half crown. She's
nere in an extasy but very seldome, once in seven
years, and thats their jubile ; and that is, when her old
stumps have by the oile of elbow-grease and continuall
drawing (for shes an excellent good carte jade) rak't

together an unexpected angell ; and then shes in her
paradice, she thinks ; for she converses now with cera-
phims. In generall, shes one of a universall conscience
or rather none at all, for she never knows the *ne plus
ultra*, the Hercules Pillar of her progging : but lets
trace her in a few particulars, *ob ovo ad malas*, I may
allude, and then you may know her by her first
aspect.

And first take her a bed (for we had need dresse
her, for she cant spare time to do it her self), and shes
a fine dirty hieroglipick of her pigsty recreations, snud-
led and kennel'd over with the dirty sackcloth of her
gloomy harding : she snorts and snores, and wakes and
scrubs, and —— and looks for day, and harkens for the
first cock ; and if it be too soon, down lies she and
streaks and picks her stincking toes, and dares not
sleep more for fear of loosing a minute. But as soon
as ever she spies the harbinger of Sol, that winged
courser, she salutes him with a χάιρε φῶς, and up rouses
nasty-nock to put on her weeds.

Her clothes, or rather those signes and representa-
tions, those faint and weak ideas of garments (for it
would poze a good scholar to distinguish and define
the difference between her and them, and the heape on
the backside Cambridge paper mil), hang about her
cadaver, her corps, her piece of clay, her all ; much
after the rate of the skin hanging about a calf when
tis half flaid, just ready to depart and take their leave

of their old mistris, whom they have served one of
Jacobs apprentiships, twice seven years ; and if the
more carelesse the more gentle behaviour she's a notable fashion monger.   Her smock and her skin are
much of the same roof, you may pick holes through
either of them ; this and her skin hath had such a
familiarity with each other, that they still play loath to
depart, for, quoth the trot, the oftener to wash boule the
sooner to rags ; its length is somewhat lesse then that of
her coats, and they and her knees, if it please you, are
equipolent, for shes very loath to be called a drags taile
slut.   But suppose a little it should so happen that a
man should extend his nerves, out of reverence to an-
tiquity, and take up her coat, her uper coat, onely
have a care of blasting neighbour and mildew, for the
extent of her placket is alwayes lower than her smock,
and that comes but an inch lower than her navel.   But
she's up and drest, well to work she hops with expedi-
tion ; her maid, if she hath one, to milk, she to hog
serving, to hacklingt, to spinning, to hempbeating, to
any thing, to hell scraping it self to get money.   And
you may know exactly her thoughts are working, for
the motion of her brains, for the most part, unloosen
her pins and erects her tippet.   Her maid coming
home, she erects her voice also, for she cannot make
haste enough, but will loose time though she flies for
it.   I would be heartily glad to see her make a cheese
once, that I might observe the speed and sluttery of

her proceeding. Well, this work done, she fals to the next, and so handles them all in order, and makes the best, worst use of her time she can possible : nay, rather then faile, she'le do two works at a time. And yet this notable dunghill raker hath scripture for what she doth, and will tell you she believes she must, and therefore doth and will provide for her family; and by this she proves she's no infidel. Well, thus much for her house : onely her dyet it is much like her self, quite out of fashion ; she bakes but once a quarter, it spends the slower ; her whey and butter-milk, etc., are her food ; she and her swine feed much alike, the difference lyes onely in the dish ; on's long, the other round.

But to know her in her finery, in her Kersmasse holiday dresse, as she calls it, take but a strict view of her visage, and you may give a shrewd guesse. Her wrinkled and withered front resembles an old fashioned pair of plateing irons ; and I believe in the dayes of yore, that was the mode of the visage. Her whole face looks like an old blasted and withered pumpkin, with a slit one way and to'ther way, and two holes of each side, for the sun hath died her fusty hide into a dark yellow, and the colour of her ruby cheeks into a bay brown.

Her hands are the clumsie hangbyes of her body ; they and their appurtenances may very well be called arms, for their hard branchey resemblance. Her fin-

N

gers, those crooked disciples of her body, stand much after the posture, as if they would denote her husbands fortune, just such crampt associates.

Her feet are inveloped in her aulean or rather cothurnian buskins, whose plodding shape and substantiall plainnesse denotes them to be intended for some hard service. Her swetty toes the *res contentæ*, the thighs contained in these swabberslops are the frankinsence of her presence, or rather the assefœtida she carryes about her to keep those she comes neer (by its nauseating odour) from sounding at her ghastly infernal presence : and now I hope you are satisfied, and I have characterized her sufficiently, you may know her by her hogo, I pray you scent her accordingly.

FINIS.

Of a Protector.

WHAT'S a Protector? He's a stately thing
  That apes it, in the nonage of a king.
A tragick actor, Cæsar in a clowne,
Hee's a brasse farthing stamped with a crown.
Æsops proud asse mask't in a lyons skin ;
An outside saint lyn'd with the devill within ;
An eccho whence the royall sound doth come,
Hee's but a barrel head unto a drum :
A bladder blown, with others breath puft full.
Not the par'lous, but perilus bull.
A counterfeited piece like one that showes
Charles his effigies with a copper nose.
Phantastick shadow of the royall head,
The brewers with the kings arms quartered.
In fine hee's one we must Protector call,
From which, the King of kings protect us all.

A Neuter Wish.

MY wishes great-
  The English fleet-
May no storme tosse-
The harpe and crosse-
Smile gentle fate-
Upon the state,-
Attend all health-
The common-wealth-
The navy of the Dutch
I all good fortune grutch ;
Vantrump and his sea forces
Shall have my daily curses,
On the Dutch admirall
The plagues of Ægypt fall.
The cavelering part,
I value not a ———.

On the death of one Mr. Pitcher.

THE worlds Architect did all our bodies frame
  To be but earthen vessels for that flame,
Which politick Prometheus stole away,
From heaven t'informe his massic lump of clay ;
By vertue of which fire our senses keep
Alive, that being put out, they fall asleep.
But if that names with nature may agree,
Our brother Pitcher rather seems to be
A water vessel, in which, death without doubt,
Water put in, and so the fire put out.
Some Puritan wit, thus would bewaile his lot,
Howle, holy sister, Pitcher's gone to pot.
But I say 'tis mortalities common show,
For Pitcher's earth, and earth must go.
We all dropt from our mother earths past wombe,
And in her bowels all must finde a tombe.
As giddy zealots often do outvie,
The weathercock, in its activity ;
Of turning round, whose brains being sore perplext,
Hug every schisme that comes in fashion next :
Then turn to the old again, when they have gone
Through all the changes of religion.
So the body after many changes must
Returne to its first principles of dust :

At last though, first we conquer many a wound ;
Death wins the field, though we must keep the
Our friend deceast had in his life time past [ground.
Grapled with many maladies, but at last,
Death or the dire physitian, one oth' twaine,
Was too hard for him, thus the proverb's plaine.
The Pitcher never goes so oft nor fast
To th' well, but it comes broken home at last.
Yet none can losse by losse of him sustaine,
Whose natures fate, tends much to others gaine ;
For death doth livelyhood to others give,
Death brake him for the nonce, all trades must live.

A Dialogue between a Tawny-more and a faire Lady.

Taw.

FIX my darke tawny starr in thy white spheare,
    Twill make thy glittring beauty shine more clear.
Lad. Your councill with the fashion suiteth not,
No ladies weare a yellow beauty spot.
Taw. I would not be a spot upon thy face,
But something in thine armes thou mights embrace.
Lad. Should herauld thy, or on my argent see
They would impute to us false armorye ;
Besides I fear infection to imbrace,
A man in my armes, with a jaundice face :

The Ægyptians on thy safron skin would pray,
And stak't to scare the crocodiles away.

Taw. If I be safron, let my seed, to yield
Encrease, be sowne within thy pleasant field.

Lad. No, pray go farme some common colony
To break up, your plow hath no share in me.

Taw. Oh but, sweet lady, tis my earnest suit,
Of this face dyde in graine, to reap the fruit.

Lad. Beyond, sea coloured sir, your suits in vaine,
I like no face dipt in an orange staine.

Taw. Slight not the surface of my orange skin,
The best part of an orange is within.
To be an orange, I could gladly choose
If you to squeeze and suck me won't refuse.

Lad. Yes, but Ile do as those that orange eat,
Hang th' peele on string when I have eat the meat.

Taw. Your skin of silver white for worth can't fellow,
Mine whose rich tincture is a golden yellow.

Lad. I praise you not, sir, for your golden hieu,
In this was Apuleas asse like you ;
But if your gold, and willing to be mine,
You shall be stampt upon to make me coyne ;
I speak my minde, yet your face would not passe,
So soon for gold, as for new scowred brasse.

Taw. My yellow sun beams thou shouldst not despise,
Sols collour when he doth in glory rise.

Lad. If your sun shine, I'le here no longer stand,
Adieu, I must be gone least I be tand.

A Petition of Questionests to Mr. Frost for their degrees, Woodcock and Heron Procters.

ALL haile, great Frost, tis our desire
   To kindle in thy breast a fire
Of gentle love ; and by our art
To thaw thy too hard frozen heart.
Be thou propitious, and we fear
No beaked procters fluttring here.
For when t's a frost, the birds we know,
Last wildnesse of and tamer grow.
We'r sirs ith house, and should we leese,
For want of wit all our degrees ;
They'l sweare a Frost hath nipt us so,
That we, like icesikles downward grow.
Thy flexile minde, I hope, will bend ;
The longest frost must have an end.
Lets have calm weather then, for though
You raigne, you will not storme, I trow.
Behold, but how our faces show
For fear of Frost as cold as snow.
Only because thou art so nice,
Chill, fear hath made's as cold as ice :
Then let's for once our pleasure have,
A common courtesie we crave :
To wit, that since such cold there haps,
Thoud'st give us leave put on our caps.

Post-script.

YOU that upon free cost this book do view,
    Suspend too harsh a censure least you shew
Your asses ears, ther's little reason why,
Judgments should be pul'd forth and purses lye
Quiet and still ; or that a man should hold
A feesimple of censure without gold.
But you that pull your purses forth and buy,   [try,
Judge till your heart strings, and your purse strings
For th' masterye, which shall crack first, soonest break,
I'le alwaies give you loosers leave to speak.

FINIS.

T. RICHARDS, 37, GREAT QUEEN STREET.

www.ingramcontent.com/pod-product-compliance
Lightning Source LLC
Chambersburg PA
CBHW031443280326
41927CB00038B/1579